T0403136

Palgrave Studies in Classical Liberalism

Series Editors
David F. Hardwick, Department of Pathology and Laboratory Medicine, The University of British Columbia, Vancouver, BC, Canada
Leslie Marsh, Department of Economics, Philosophy and Political Science, The University of British Columbia, Okanagan, BC, Canada

This series offers a forum to writers concerned that the central presuppositions of the liberal tradition have been severely corroded, neglected, or misappropriated by overly rationalistic and constructivist approaches.

The hardest-won achievement of the liberal tradition has been the wrestling of epistemic independence from overwhelming concentrations of power, monopolies and capricious zealotries. The very precondition of knowledge is the exploitation of the epistemic virtues accorded by society's situated and distributed manifold of spontaneous orders, the DNA of the modern civil condition.

With the confluence of interest in situated and distributed liberalism emanating from the Scottish tradition, Austrian and behavioral economics, non-Cartesian philosophy and moral psychology, the editors are soliciting proposals that speak to this multidisciplinary constituency. Sole or joint authorship submissions are welcome as are edited collections, broadly theoretical or topical in nature.

Nils Karlson

Reviving Classical Liberalism Against Populism

palgrave
macmillan

Nils Karlson
RATIO
Stockholm, Sweden

ISSN 2662-6470 ISSN 2662-6489 (electronic)
Palgrave Studies in Classical Liberalism
ISBN 978-3-031-49073-6 ISBN 978-3-031-49074-3 (eBook)
https://doi.org/10.1007/978-3-031-49074-3

Cover illustration: © Pattadis Walarput/Alamy Stock Photo

This Palgrave Macmillan imprint is published by the registered company Springer Nature Switzerland AG
The registered company address is: Gewerbestrasse 11, 6330 Cham, Switzerland

Paper in this product is recyclable.

Preface

Populism poses a threat to liberty, free markets, and the open society on all continents. How can this development be explained and what can be done about it? These are puzzles that have given rise to many discussions with colleagues and friends in recent years. I thank them all for helping me to write this book.

To my knowledge this book is the first to analyze populism from the perspective of classical liberalism; in presenting a synthesized explanatory model for how both left-wing and right-wing populists promote autocratization; in tracing the ideational roots of the core populist ideas; to show that these ideas form a collectivistic identity politics; and to present distinctive strategies of how liberals can fight back against the populist threat. I argue that this requires the revival of liberalism itself by defending and developing the liberal institutions, the liberal spirit, liberal narratives, and liberal statecraft. An extensive list of counterstrategies against populism is presented and discussed.

I am highly grateful for the valuable comments on earlier versions of the full manuscript by Mark Pennington, Paul Lewis, John Meadowcroft, Pavel Kuchar, Samuel De Canio, and Bryan Cheang at the Department of Political Economy, King's College, London, and by Andreas Bergh, Niclas Elert, and Andreas Johansson Heinö in Stockholm, Sweden. In addition, I have also benefitted from comments by participants at public lectures and presentations about the theme of the book in Bretton Woods, London, Oslo, Lund, and Stockholm.

The major parts of this book were written during my time as a visiting fellow at the Hoover Institution, Stanford University, during the winter and spring of 2022. It is an outstanding research environment, with excellent facilities, libraries, seminars, and colleagues. Without these resources the book could not have been written. I am highly grateful to Director Condoleezza Rice and Professor John Taylor for inviting me. I am equally grateful to the Ratio Institute in Stockholm, and its Chair Marie Rudberg and Director Charlotta Stern, for the liberty to pursue the research behind the book for an extended period.

Lastly, I want to thank Magnus Bergvalls Stiftelse and Helge Ax:son Johnsons stiftelse for the financial support during my visit to Stanford.

Stockholm, Sweden   Nils Karlson
August 2023

Praise for *Reviving Classical Liberalism Against Populism*

"George Orwell famously warned that the future of humanity was one of the giant boot of the state stamping on its face. It doesn't matter if the boot is on the left or right foot when it does the stamping. Nils Karlson's important and timely book, *Reviving Classical Liberalism Against Populism* lays bare the consequences for peace and prosperity of the 'us vs them' mentality of both left-wing and right-wing populism that has seemingly swept the globe in the past decade. Karlson gives us plausible reasons for this rise, as well as suggestions on how to reverse this trend in our political life through the revival of a full-throated classical liberalism. But liberals, he insists, must learn the hard lesson — a lesson I would add that James Buchanan also stressed — that rational policy deliberation over economic growth and development is not enough. We must, as Buchanan put it, put the soul back into classical liberalism. Karlson stresses that modern adherents of a true liberal society must understand that individuals seek belonging, community, meaning, and emancipation, and in that recognition than craft a liberal order that promotes self-development and human flourishing. Read this book, absorb its lessons, and get busy crafting a radical liberalism fit for our age."

—Peter Boettke, *Professor of Economics and Philosophy, George Mason University, USA*

"Authoritarian populism has emerged as the most dangerous political virus to attack the values and institutions of liberty over the past generation. Across the world—from the United States to Turkey, from India to Israel—the virus has spread, with devastating consequences for the functionality and prestige of liberal democracies. It has weakened the free world and empowered the agents of oppression and brutality in China, Iran, and Russia. How has authoritarian populism managed to gnaw its way into the soft tissue of democratic societies? Why has it proven to be so pernicious? And how can classical liberal ideas and institutions fight back and defeat the populist virus? In Reviving Classical Liberalism against Populism Nils Karlson tackles these questions with expertise and aplomb. A must read for anyone concerned to defend liberal democracies from the menace of authoritarian populism."

—Amichai Magen, *Lauder School of Government, Diplomacy, and Strategy, Reichman University, Herzliya, Israel, and Freeman-Spogli Institute for International Studies, Stanford University, USA*

"One of today's most pressing issues for classical liberals—and for centrists more generally—is the threat of populism. Nils Karlson's book clarifies this oftentimes elusive concept and provides crucial inspirations for the embattled political center how to deal with populists from the left and the right."

—Stefan Kolev, *Ludwig Erhard Forum for Economy and Society, Berlin, and professor of political economy at the University of Applied Sciences Zwickau, Germany*

"This book is an appeal to classical liberals to defend democracy and freedom against the populist pandemic which had been spreading everywhere in the last twenty years. The author, Nils Karlson, an outstanding classical liberal scholar, provides a breathtaking analysis of the autocratic direction of populism coming from both left and right that challenges democratic institutions through its rhetorical style.

Karlson explains how today's classical liberals may fight back against the threat of populism. He proposes counterstrategies able to develop new policies and to build up a new liberal narrative aimed to reinforce the spirit of a liberal society: no longer simply based on the principle of no-harm, rather focused on the "liberal spirit". Moral pluralism, mutual respect, the promotion of federalism, decentralization, and social mobility are the pillars of classical liberalism: they shaped a civil and open society and we need them back. We need to read this book."

—Giandomenica Becchio, *Professor of history of economic thought, methodology of economics, and theory of entrepreneurship at the University of Torino (ESOMAS Department), Italy*

"After his great book Statecraft and liberal reform in advanced democracies, Professor Karlson is back with a new essay. A book devoted to the defense of liberal democracy and an open society. A work that attacks the greatest threat facing free systems today: Populism in its different forms. His analysis faces a definition of the phenomenon, a description of its perverse way of working, and a potential response to protect our freedom. The easy, superficial, demagogic, and authoritarian politics that define populism profoundly threaten liberal democratic systems. But above all, populism threatens the structure of rights and freedoms of people, who, immersed in everyday life, do not clearly perceive how populists erode the institutions that serve as a protection barrier. The answer offered by Professor Karlson is freedom, the Rule of Law, decentralization, and deconcentration of power. In short, the need to recover and promote classical liberal politics by generating new narratives that permeate society. His work values the liberal ideas that have sustained a large number of nations during the nineteenth, twentieth and twenty-first centuries. A work that is worth reading and that shows, once again, the commitment that Nils Karlson has with the defense of freedom and open societies."

—Eduardo Fernández Luiña, *Associate Professor Universidad Francisco Marroquín, Guatemala*

"One cannot fight the collectivistic identity politics of populism with cost-benefit studies and policy analysis alone. As Nils Karlson argues in his riveting, essential book, the arts, and the humanities, "emotions... ethos ... narratives," are necessary to save us from 1984 in 2024."

—Deirdre McCloskey, *Professor Emerita of Economics, History, English, and Communication, University of Illinois at Chicago, USA*

"Classical liberalism is better than populism, flat out. Nils Karlson will tell you why, both for the US and Sweden, and for the broader world."

—Tyler Cowen, *Professor of Economics, George Mason University, USA*

CONTENTS

1 Classical Liberalism Against Populism   1
References   4

2 Populism: Defining Characteristics   7
Unserious and Ill-Founded Policies   8
A Rhetorical Style and Discourse Frame   10
Left- and Right-Wing Populism   12
An Autocratic Institutional Orientation   15
The Populist Strategies   17
References   18

3 A Threat to Liberty, Free Markets, and the Open Society   21
Populist Voter Support   22
Democratic Backsliding   23
A Worldwide Illiberal Turn   24
References   25

4 Explaining Populism and Autocratization   27
Analyzing Populism as Autocratic Institutional Change   28
Globalization, Immigration, and Policy Failures   30
Culture and Identity   35
Psychology and Human Nature   37

Social Media and Echo Chambers — 38
Charismatic Leaders and Policy Entrepreneurs — 39
Explaining Populist Institutional Change — 40
References — 41

5 The Populist Divisive, Activist Ideas — 47
A Politics of Resentment and Recognition — 48
The Ideas Behind the Populist Strategies — 49
Identity as a Function of Meaning, Community, and Virtue — 53
Meaning — 54
Community — 56
Virtue — 57
A Collectivistic Identity Politics — 59
References — 62

6 The Classical Liberal Ideas, Predicaments, and Potentials — 67
The Liberal Predicaments — 68
The Three Dimensions of Classical Liberalism — 69
The Liberal Institutions — 70
The Liberal Economy and Society — 72
The Liberal Spirit — 73
The Liberal Potentials — 75
References — 75

7 Expose the Populist Strategies and Their Consequences — 79
References — 81

8 Defend and Develop the Liberal Institutions — 83
Improve Liberal Literacy — 84
Secure a Strong, Limited, and Decent State — 87
Support Federalism and Decentralization — 90
Stimulate Social Mobility — 90
Strengthen Integration — 93
Restore Public Discourse — 96
References — 97

9 Embrace and Promote the Liberal Spirit — 101
Meaning, Community, and Virtue in a Liberal Society — 102
A Politics of Tolerance, Recognition, and Human
Flourishing — 104
A Collective Legitimizing Identity? — 108

Create Liberal Narratives   109
References   112

10 Develop Liberal Statecraft   115
References   118

11 A Classical Liberal Revival   121
Reference   125

Index   127

LIST OF TABLES

Table 2.1 Ways that populists frame the 'us-versus-them' logic   13
Table 2.2 Varieties of populism   15
Table 2.3 The major populist strategies   17

CHAPTER 1

Classical Liberalism Against Populism

Abstract This chapter introduces and summarizes the major themes, arguments, and contributions of this book. How can liberals and classical liberals fight back against the populist threat to liberty, free markets, and the open society? I explore the defining characteristics of populism, to make populism intelligible, recognizable, and contestable. I explain the ideational background of the populist ideas and strategies and show how populists promote their non-liberal institutional changes through the deliberate polarization of society and a collectivistic identity politics. Based on this analysis several counterstrategies are developed that require a revival of classical liberalism.

Keywords Populism · Autocracy · Threats to liberty · Polarization · Liberalism · Classical liberalism

After the fall of the Soviet Union and the Berlin wall waves of liberalization spread worldwide. Markets were opened, taxes lowered, and regulations cut. Liberalism was winning and the number of democracies increased.

But in the last decade, the trend turned. According to one assessment, the level of democracy enjoyed by the average global citizen is down to 1986 levels. Liberty and the rule of law are threatened in many countries.

© The Author(s) 2024
N. Karlson, *Reviving Classical Liberalism Against Populism*,
Palgrave Studies in Classical Liberalism,
https://doi.org/10.1007/978-3-031-49074-3_1

72 percent of the world population—or 5,7 billion people—today lives in different sorts of autocracies. Just ten years ago it was only 46 percent (V-Dem Institute, 2022). How could this happen?

A major reason behind this development, I shall argue, is the emergence of populism as a threat to free markets, democracy, and liberal, open societies. A populist, authoritarian pandemic has been spreading in Europe and the US, in Latin America, Asia, and Africa. This threat to liberty is different from those of the twentieth century. Socialism and communism in the traditional sense of state ownership of the means of production and central planning of the whole economy have only survived in marginalized countries like North Korea and Cuba. The same is largely true for fascism, interpreted as ultra-nationalistic, totalitarian regimes with dictatorial power that forcibly suppress opposition, and regiment society and the economy hierarchically, arguably with the exceptions of today's autocratic Russia and China.

Populism is more deceptive. It emerges within democracies. It is not an ideology in the standard sense, even though it has distinct characteristics. In fact, it is compatible with most traditional ideologies, except liberalism I shall argue, and represents a political dimension that goes in another direction than the traditional scale that we are accustomed to. Rather, populism is based on divisive, activist ideas that form the basis for a specific set of political strategies, which use a rhetorical style and discursive frame to gain power and change the institutional structure of society in a non-liberal, autocratic direction. In essence, populism is a kind of collectivistic identity politics that comes from both left and right.

How can we explain this development? What can be done about it? How can liberals and classical liberals fight back against this threat to the free world? These are the main themes in this book.

I set out to explore the defining characteristics of populism, to make populism intelligible, recognizable, and contestable. I shall explain the ideational background of the populist ideas and strategies and show how populists promote their non-liberal institutional changes through the deliberate polarization of society and a collectivistic identity politics.

The purpose is also to discuss how liberals and liberalism can fight back against this threat to the free world. Such counterstrategies involve a reviving of the ideas of liberalism itself, including the defense of liberal institutions and the development of new and better policies to batter some of the most important shortcomings that our societies are facing. A major argument will be that rational arguments and institutional improvements will not be enough. Liberals also need to be better at using arguments based on emotions and character, about the ethos or spirit of a liberal society, as well as improved narratives to succeed. A liberal politics of identity need to be advanced as part of a developed liberal statecraft.

By "liberal" and "liberalism" I mean classical liberal. The terms liberal and classical liberal will be used interchangeably. Occasionally I shall nevertheless also refer to social liberalism, sometimes for appraisal, sometimes for criticism. For a discussion of different interpretations of liberalism, see e.g., Gray (1986), Fawcett (2018).

Classical liberalism is usually presented as an ideological position that favors individual liberty and dignity, limited government, the rule of law, property rights, civil rights, freedom of association, pluralism, constitutional democracy, minority rights, a private sphere, and sound money. Classical liberals believe that the only good reason to restrict people's freedom is to prevent them from doing harm to others. But liberalism also favors free markets and civil society, with competition, entrepreneurship, voluntary organizations, clubs, and families – the consequences of liberal principles and institutions. Just as important, but often forgotten or disregarded, is what I shall call the "liberal spirit". Classical liberals rejoice in individual development and self-authorship, entrepreneurship, diversity and tolerance, moral pluralism, mutual respect, free speech and rational discourse, science, in different virtues, and human flourishing. Together these dimensions of liberalism reinforce each other.

The book is written within the tradition of political theory and institutional economics, but I will use a wide variety of sources, including results and analyses from social psychology, ethics, law, and history. It is an idea analysis and offers a kind of analytical narrative (Bates et al., 1998).

In Chapter 2 the defining characteristics of populism in previous are discussed and synthesized. It is argued that populism has three modes: unserious and ill-founded policies; a rhetorical style and discursive frame; and an autocratic institutional orientation. Varieties of populism are discussed, and the major populist strategies are presented. This is followed by a short Chapter 3 where the actual support for populist parties and regimes, and their threats to democracy, liberty, and the open society are summarized. Next, in Chapter 4, the most popular, but partial, explanations that have been proposed for why and how populists succeed in promoting autocratic institutional change are discussed and synthesized into "a populist model of autocratization". My conclusion is that populist ideas, beliefs, and values that form populist strategies play the central role in this process of institutional autocratization.

In the following Chapter 5, the ideational roots of these divisive, activist ideas are traced back to thinkers like Jean-Jacques Rousseau, Friedrich Nietzsche, Martin Heidegger, and Carl Schmitt, later to be developed within post-modernism and critical theory, to form the basis for both left- and right-wing populism. It is argued that populism offers meaning and a sense of belonging to its followers, a kind of collectivistic identity politics.

In Chapter 6 classical liberalism, its three dimensions, and different liberal predicaments and potentials to fight back against populism are explored. In the following chapters, 7 to 10, different liberal counter-strategies against the populist threats are presented and discussed under four broad headings:

- Expose the populist strategies and their consequences.
- Defend and develop the liberal institutions
- Embrace and promote the liberal spirit
- Develop liberal statecraft

Liberal statecraft should promote not only a liberal economy but just as important a civil and open society, and perhaps most importantly the liberal spirit. This requires the conquering of the idea arena, the promotion of liberal policy entrepreneurs, and the investment in power resources that can change institutions and policies. It is a polycentric effort where many different actors and policy entrepreneurs need to be involved.

The last Chapter 11 summarizes my conclusions by asking for a revival of liberalism itself.

REFERENCES

Bates, R. H., Greif, A., Levi, M., Rosenthal, J.-L., & Weingast, B. R. (1998). *Analytic narratives*. Princeton University Press.

Fawcett, E. (2018). *Liberalism: The life of an idea* (2nd edition). Princeton: Princeton University Press.

Gray, J. (1986). *Liberalism*. Minneapolis, MN: University of Minnesota Press.

V-Dem Institute. (2022). *Defiance in the face of autocratization*. Democracy report 2022. https://www.v-dem.net/documents/29/V-dem_democracyrep ort2023_lowres.pdf

CHAPTER 2

Populism: Defining Characteristics

Abstract This chapter explores and synthesizes the defining characteristics of left- and right-wing populism in previous research. In conclusion, populism has three modes. A first that emphasizes the use of unserious and ill-founded policy solutions to complex social and economic problems, and a second that focuses on a specific set of political strategies which use a distinct rhetorical style and discursive frame to deliberately polarize society, and a third that stresses the autocratic institutional orientation that follows. The three modes often go together and form the political strategies that populists use.

Keywords Populism · Defining characteristics · Populist strategies · Unserious policies · Polarization · Autocratic orientation · Left- and rightwing populism

There is today a huge, expanding literature in the social sciences about populism. After having surveyed the major empirical and theoretical contributions, an obvious conclusion is that it is hard to define populism. It comes in many shades, some to the left and some to the right, but also in the center. As pointed out by Taggart (2000), populism is like a chameleon, adapting to the colors of the environment, local and ideological. Hence, as noted above, populism is not an ideology in the traditional

N. Karlson, *Reviving Classical Liberalism Against Populism*,
Palgrave Studies in Classical Liberalism,
https://doi.org/10.1007/978-3-031-49074-3_2

sense like liberalism, conservatism, or socialism. It does not have a distinct set of core values and beliefs about how the world works or a particular view of human nature. Moreover, there are degrees of populism. Consequently, I shall instead of attempting to give a strict definition provide some defining characteristics of populism and populists.

Simplifying, populism may be said to have three modes. In popular discourse and among economists' populism is often seen as a politics that appeals to the people by advocating unserious and ill-founded policies. However, in the broader social science literature populism has increasingly become identified with a distinct set of political strategies that deliberately cultivate the polarization of society. As we shall see, these first two modes often go together, resulting in the third, a process of creeping autocratization. This is when populism becomes a real threat to liberal democracy, markets, and the open society.

Unserious and Ill-Founded Policies

Populists are thus often, especially by economists, considered to offer unserious and ill-founded policy solutions to complex social and economic problems, often some sort of economic or social crises, to get elected. Or more generally, offering simplistic answers to complex questions. Typical examples of this mode are major increases in public spending and redistribution at the same time as advocating tax cuts or favoring severe punishments as the sole measure to battle crime or juvenile pregnancies.

For example, Williamson (1992: 347) defined populism as "the phenomenon where a politician tries to win power ... with sweeping promises of benefits and concessions ... to the lower classes". Dornbusch and Edwards (1991) defined it as a set of economic policies aimed at redistributing income by implementing policies that violate 'good economics', including budget constraints and efficiency principles. Similarly, Rodrik (2018: 196) sees populism as a set of "irresponsible, unsustainable policies that often end in disaster and hurt most ordinary people they purportedly aim to help". These kinds of policies are a major factor contributing to the often-observed economic decline under populist rule (Dornbusch & Edwards, 1991; Dovis et al., 2016).

In an analysis of more than 20 experiences or episodes of populism in Latin America from 1946 to 2019—including the regimes of Juan Peron in Argentine, Salvador Allende in Chile, Rafael Correa in Ecuador, Hugo Chavez and Nicolás Maduro in Venezuela, and Jair Bolsonaro in

Brazil—Edwards (2010) distinguishes between five phases that may be summarized as follows:

1. The election or rise of a charismatic leader who advocates heterodox economic policies to redistribute income, explicitly ignoring constraints on public expenditures and monetary expansion.
2. The economy reacts strongly to aggregate demand shock; and growth, real wages, and employment are high.
3. The economy runs into bottlenecks due to expansionary demand, lack of foreign currency, and capital flight; inflation increases significantly, wages are indexed, and budget deficits continue to worsen.
4. Pervasive shortages, increased capital flights, and an extreme acceleration of inflation; price controls are intensified, and the currency is devalued.
5. Collapse, and cleanup by a new government, often through the enactment of an International Monetary Fund program.

In the more recent examples of populism that he documents, inflation did not soar to the same extent, while public debt instead exploded, and protectionist policies, mandatory minimum wages increase, and constitutional reforms were implemented. Nevertheless, in all cases, as a result of the populist policies, the real incomes—and in particular the incomes of the poor—declined to levels significantly lower than when the populist episodes started. Moreover, the institutions of democracy and the open society were undermined. Significantly, 13 of these 20 experiences involved left-wing governments (see also Cachanosky & Padilla, 2021).

In an extensive historical study by Funke et al. (2020) a quantitative evaluation of 50 populist regimes from 1900 to 2018 was carried out, showing that the populists underperform significantly: 15 years after the populist takeover, GDP per capita was 10% below the non-populist counterfactual, and income inequality did not fall. Rising economic nationalism and protectionism, unsustainable macroeconomic policies, and institutional decay under populist rule did lasting damage to the economies.

A Rhetorical Style and Discourse Frame

In sociology and political science, populism is instead often characterized as a specific political style, discourse frame or strategy, designed to mobilize the deserving majority (the 'people') against, allegedly, corrupt, conspiring elites and the institutions they occupy. From this mode or perspective, populism may be presented as a seemingly democratic device. Müller (2016) among others, however, argues that it often hides dangerously anti-democratic impulses which can stray into authoritarianism.

The deliberate polarization of politics and society is at the core of this strategy, using emotional arguments and framing to create anger and moral outrage toward opponents and their supporters (Prior & van Hoef, 2018). On this interpretation, the active promotion of political conflict is central to populism. The polarization of politics and society into an'us versus them' antagonism is the deliberate means used to mobilize support. Often a real or imagined economic or social crisis of some kind, increasing uncertainty, is used to trigger such sentiments. The two modes of populism may thus develop together.

It has been argued that it is possible to distinguish between ideational, political-strategical, and socio-cultural approaches to the concept of populism (Kaltwasser et al., 2017), but in my view, they can all be viewed as characterizing populism as a specific kind of political strategy with a specific institutional orientation, namely, to seek polarization to promote autocratization. By political strategy is here simply meant a plan for how to gain power and stay in power.

The populists thus portray or frame themselves as the true democrats and the representatives of the people against the elites (Mudde 2004; Müller, 2016), whether political, economic, or cultural, often called "the establishment". Populists also most often identify, or create, external enemies, 'others', whom they blame for the shortcomings of their own societies. It could be immigrants, Romani, or Jews, or even foreign or supranational powers like the World Bank, the European Union, international corporations, or the globalized economy itself. According to Galston (2017), this means that a kind of tribalism is typical for populist movements.

According to Mudde (2007), populism moreover claims that politics should be an expression of the *volonté general* (general will) of the people, based on the ideas of Rousseau. Consequently, populists do not believe in constitutional constraints on democratic processes or the rights of minorities against the will of the majority. Populists dislike the check-and-balances of liberal democracy (Urbinati, 2019) and are anti-pluralists (Galston, 2017). Populists are ultra-majoritarian. The 'people' that populist appeal to are at most a majority of the voters, as Urbinati (2019) has pointed out. According to Diamond (2019), populism thus has four core features: anti-elitist; anti-institutional; plebiscitary, and ultra-majoritarian. Populists in this way aim to create a direct connection with their supporters, unmediated by political parties, civil society groups, or the media, using mass meetings, television shows, and digital channels.

Populist leaders are often seen as charismatic demagogues who have an intuitive sense for using this'us versus them' logic in media and in speeches (Eichengreen, 2018). As the 'true' representatives of the people, they prefer to communicate directly to people on television, mass meetings, press conferences, and, nowadays, social media platforms, without interfering filters or commentators. Kenny (2017) explicitly understands populism as a distinctively personalistic type of political movement or organization in which charismatic leaders look to directly mobilize mass constituencies through the media and other means.

Typically, populists also deliberately show crude, ruthless, unrestrained, "bad boy" manners (Moffitt, 2016). Ostiguy (2017) has called this "flaunting of the 'low'" in politics, to show that the populist leaders themselves come from the people. This is in contrast with the 'high' style of the established elites, in which public self-presentation is well-mannered, proper, and composed. For example, Rodrigo Duterte, the former, popular president of the Philippines, not only pioneered a brutal tough-on-crime policy involving extrajudicial killings of alleged criminals, but also bragged about extramarital affairs and, on separate occasions, referred to both the US President and the Pope as a "Son of a Whore" (Beauchamp, 2022). Donald Trump in the US arguably showed the same kind of "bad boy" manors in his attacks on opponents, media, and the courts, just as Hugo Chavez in Venezuela and many others (Ostiguy & Roberts, 2016).

At the same time, populist leaders also need to signal that they somehow are above and better than the people and therefore deserve to rule and represent them (Moffitt, 2016). Various techniques are used to show such extraordinariness, including showing off wealth, and masculinity, and presenting themselves as the singular figure who can fix the economy and the law and order, etc. Ultimately, populist leaders see themselves as symbols, embodying the true people. As put by Hugo Chavez: "I am the people" (Zúquete, 2008).

Apart from promises of policies of the kinds described in the previous section, populists usually have strong opinions about how their societies should be, depending on their ideological leanings. For conservatives, it may concern the promotion of traditional values, for socialists it may be the equality of resources. They are willing to use the state to promote the "good" or the values they favor through taxes, regulations, and interventions in markets and civil society. Individual rights are subordinated to the "common good", or general will, as interpreted by the populist leadership.

The rhetorical styles or discourse frames of populists involve the use of narratives that "construct" the people and their different enemies. Emotions of belonging and identity, rather than rational arguments about facts and empirical evidence, are central to these populist strategies. The narratives typically involve a demand for respect and recognition of the lives of ordinary, hard-working people, who are said to be left behind and ignored by the elites and established institutions.'Facts' and 'news' are constructed and contrasted to the 'lies' of opponents, or the 'fake news' of the media.

To some extent, all politics in democratic societies have some of these elements of populism in it, a fact that often can be observed in heated election campaigns and the like when opponents attack each other. However, populists are willing to use the kind of strategies and narratives described above to the extreme. While not in any sense democratic, the same is true of autocratic regimes like Putin's Russia and Xi Jinping's China.

As we shall see in a coming chapter, these populist strategies are based on several divisive, activist ideas and the deliberate denial of rational discourse, objectivity, and truth. These ideas originate from Friedrich Nietzsche, Martin Heidegger, and Carl Schmitt, later to be developed by thinkers within post-modernism and critical theory, to form the basis for both left- and right-wing populism.

LEFT- AND RIGHT-WING POPULISM

There are both left- and right-wing versions of how populists frame the 'us-versus-them' logic. Those on the left commonly argue that" neoliberalism" is to blame for all kinds of economic and social problems. According to this rhetorical framing, it was the deregulations, privatizations, and tax cuts starting in the 1980s that are the causes of all kinds of problems within education and healthcare systems, with consequences like inequality, a precariat, etc. An overall theme in this construct is that neoliberalism has enabled huge transnational corporations to use the state (especially in the US) to promote their own interests (see e.g., Cayla, 2021; Elliott, 2021; Harvey, 2007; Mirowski & Plehwe, 2009). I shall return to the question of neoliberalism in Chapter 6.

Those on the right instead blame liberalism more generally for causing threats to traditional family values, religion, and communities. In their narrative, it is untrammeled markets, competition, choice, "identity politics", LGBTQ rights, abortion rights, etc., but also immigrants, Islam, etc., that cause the threats to national culture and to social and economic stability (see e.g., Deneen 2018; Hazony, 2018). Table 2.1 summarizes how left-wing and right-wing populists frame the 'us-versus-them' logic (partly inspired by Kyle & Gultchin, 2018).

Right-wing populist strategies thus differ to some extent from those on the left, even though they use the same kind of strategy. As shown in the table they differ in how they construct the people, the elite, and the 'others', and in the key themes they emphasize. But the structure of how they go about creating polarization is largely similar.

The left-wing populist parties and politicians, like the Podemos in Spain, Syriza in Greece, and all their Latin American counterparts, all

Table 2.1 Ways that populists frame the 'us-versus-them' logic

	Left-wing populism	*Right-wing populism*
The 'people'	The working class, ordinary, decent people, welfare recipients, the "precariat"	'Native' citizens, patriots, often rural and religious, ordinary, hardworking people, taxpayers
The 'elite'	Neoliberals, right-wing media, right of center political parties, experts, capitalists, IMF, World Bank	Academics, experts, left-wing media, established parties, international organizations, EU, cosmopolitan elites
The 'others'	Big business, capital owners, foreign companies, actors on the global markets, US, EU	Migrants, non-natives, ethnic and religious minorities, Muslims, Jews
Key themes	Anti-capitalism, anti-globalization, neoliberalism, exploitation, protectionism, anti-Americanism, inequality, redistribution, restoring welfare systems	Nationalism, cultural identity, anti-immigration, traditionalism, law and order, anti-globalization, national sovereignty, protectionism, restoring welfare systems

use classical Marxist and socialist ways of framing capitalists, big business, capitalist institutions, globalization, and the like as the enemies of the 'people', the working class, with common themes around inequality, redistribution, and welfare. Bernie Sanders in the US and Jeremy Corbyn in the UK are two well-known examples. This is the kind of rhetorical style that socialists and many social democratic parties have used for the last 100 years or more.

The right-wing populist parties and politicians, on the other hand, as the Lega in Italy, Fidesz in Hungary, the National Rally (National Front before 2018) in France, United Kingdom Independence Party, UKIP in the UK, Alternative für Deutschland, AFD, in Germany, Law and Justice party, PiS, in Poland, Freiheitliche Partei Österreichs, FPÖ, in Austria, and the Swedish Democrats in Sweden, but also Trump in the US, Bolsonaro in Brazil, Erdoğan in Turkey, and many others, are nativist or nationalists that frame experts, established parties, left-wing media, international organizations, cosmopolitan elites, immigrants, ethnic and religious minorities as enemies of the people. Common themes among these are nationalism, protectionism, anti-pluralism, cultural identity, law and order, traditional values, and the restoration of welfare systems.

In a slightly similar way, Kyle and Gultchin (2018) have distinguished between three types of populism: (1) "cultural populists" that claim that the true people are the native members of the nation-state and with outsiders such as immigrants, criminals, ethnic and religious minorities, and cosmopolitan elites; (2) "socio-economic populists" that claim that the true people are honest, hard-working members of the working class, and outsiders that include big business, capital owners and actors perceived as propping up an international capitalist system; and (3) "anti-establishment populists" that paint the true people as hard-working victims of a state run by special interests and outsiders as political elites. In all cases, including those in the center, the populist parties adapt to the local conditions.

Norris (2020), based on a global expert survey, differentiates between the economic and social values of different types of populist parties, which gives a more nuanced view than the simple left–right dimension. In Table 2.2 some examples are given:

Table 2.2 Varieties of populism

	Left-wing economic values	*Right-wing economic values*
Conservative social values	Hungary's Fidesz, Polish Law and Justice party, Danish People's Party	Swiss People's Party, Israel's Likud, India's *Bharatiya Janata Party*, BJP, Greek Golden Dawn, US Republicans
Liberal social values	Spain's Podemos, Greece's Syrzia, Italy's Five Star Movement	Bangladesh Jatiya Party, Norway Progress Party

For example, Poland's Law and Justice party (in common with many Eastern European populist parties) is leftwing towards the economy and welfare state but highly traditional in its social values, regarding Christianity, homosexuality, and immigrants. By contrast, fewer populist parties are seen by experts as free market economically and socially liberal, but there are some, such as the Norwegian Progress party. The position of several of the parties mentioned can of course be discussed. It is worth noting as well that some populist parties or movements are hard to classify as either left or right. They may be at the very center of politics, both economically and socially, but they may also be formed from a completely different standpoint, e.g., as Islamist parties, that use exactly the same kind of strategies as those described above.

An Autocratic Institutional Orientation

When populists get into power the rhetorical style and discourse frames tend to be used to implement successive autocratic measures, like limiting the opposition through manipulating elections, thwarting the free press, changing the constitution in their own favor, and circumscribing minority, civil, political, and economic rights.

This should come as no surprise, given the populists' anti-pluralism, their belief that established elites or the opposition per definition are treasonous, and their conviction that they represent the general will of the people. Since they represent the true people, other people's votes do not count as legitimate. This autocratic orientation is what makes populism a real threat to liberal democracy and an open society. This is also why populist tendencies and the use of populist strategies by established democratic parties and actors may have long-run dangerous effects on our societies.

As argued by Krygier et al. (2022), it is common for populists to weaken or dismantle legal and constitutional checks upon executive and/ or legislative powers, thus distorting and typically seeking to subvert democratic and constitutional rules of the game, but not by abolishing them wholesale. The public institutions, just like the public radio and television services, are filled with loyal supporters, while their private counterparts become controlled by various clients of the populist regimes.

This autocratic institutional orientation is prevalent on both the left and the right, as examples from Latin America and Eastern Europe show (V-Dem Institute, 2022). For example, as Weyland (2013) has shown, in Latin America democracy has been on the defensive under the cover of progressive rhetoric with leaders like Hugo Chávez who eroded institutional checks and balances, marginalized the opposition through discriminatory legalism, and severely skewed political competition. The same is true of more right-wing leaders like Victor Orbán in Hungary and Recep Tayyip Erdoğan in Turkey.

Populists are thus usually not against electoral democracy per se, but rather at odds with liberal democracy (Mudde & Kaltwasser, 2012, 2017). They are hostile to the underlying values and principles of constitution-alism, and to institutional practices that have been developed to serve those values and principles, while elections are still held, and repeatedly so, to boost the legitimacy of the regime (Levitsky & Ziblatt, 2018). Usually, these authoritarian ambitions are not proclaimed openly, but, as many know, in 2014 Hungarian prime minister Viktor Orbán openly declared his vision for an "illiberal democracy", based on a strong state, a weak opposition, and emaciated checks and balances (Belov, 2021). This means the end of liberty and an open society.

Diamond (2019) has described this process as "the autocrats' twelve-step program":

1. Begin to demonize the opposition as illegitimate and unpatriotic.
2. Undermine the independence of the courts.
3. Attack the independence of the media.
4. Gain control of any public broadcasting.
5. Impose strict control of the internet.
6. Subdue other elements of civil society.
7. Intimidate the business community.
8. Enrich a new class of crony capitalists.
9. Assert political control over the civil service and the security apparatus.

10. Gerrymander districts and rig the electoral rules.

12. Gain control of the body that runs the elections.

13. Repeat steps 1– 1.

THE POPULIST STRATEGIES

To summarize, in my interpretation populism has three modes: a first that emphasizes the use of unserious and ill-founded policy solutions to complex social and economic problems, and a second that focuses on a specific set of political strategies which use a distinct rhetorical style and discursive frame to deliberately polarize society, and a third that stresses the autocratic institutional orientation that follows. The three modes often go together forming the political strategies that populists use.

Table 2.3 summarizes the main characteristics of the major populist strategies under two headings: rhetorical style and discursive frame, and autocratic orientation.

Table 2.3   The major populist strategies

A.	**Rhetorical style and discursive framing**
1.	Use any kind of crisis or major economic and social changes to delegitimize established parties and elites
2.	Promote unserious and ill-founded policy solutions
3.	Portray yourself and your movement as the symbolic representative of the'true people'
4.	Foster polarization, use the 'us-versus-them' logic, attack the establishment and different elites
5.	Identify 'others' that threatens the existential identity of the 'true people'
6.	Demonize opponents, attack media and science for producing lies and fake news
7.	Flaunt the 'low', be intolerant and ruthless
8.	Use narratives and emotional arguments about identity, rather than rational arguments and evidence, and call for the respect for and recognition of ordinary people
B.	**Autocratic institutional orientation**
1.	Create a direct relationship with the 'people' through charismatic leadership and by circumventing representative government
2.	Take control of the courts, the public service, media companies, and restrict media freedom
3.	Manipulate elections, abolish minority rights, constitutional constraints, and the rule of law to establish an illiberal democracy
4.	Use the power of the state to promote your own ideas of the good
5.	Favor creeping autocratization, the gradual decline of the democratic, open society, rather than open coups

References

Beauchamp, Z. (2022). *The Philippine election is the latest example of illiberalism's popularity.* Vox. https://www.vox.com/2022/5/17/23068682/marcos-dut erte-philippine-election-2022-illiberalism

Belov, M. (Ed.). (2021). *Populist constitutionalism and illiberal democracies: Between constitutional imagination, normative entrenchment and political reality.* Intersentia Ltd.

Cachanosky, N., & Padilla, A. (2021). Left-populism, commodity prices, and economic crises in Latin America. *Journal of Private Enterprise, 36*(Summer 20), 1–17.

Cayla, D. (2021). *Populism and neoliberalism.* Routledge.

Deneen, P. (2018). *Why liberalism failed.* Yale University Press.

Diamond, L. (2019). *Ill winds: Saving democracy from Russian rage, Chinese ambition, and American complacency.* Penguin Press.

Dornbusch, R., & Edwards, S. (1991). *The macroeconomics of Latin American populism.* University of Chicago Press for the NBER.

Dovis, A., Golosov, M., & Shourideh, A. (2016). Political economy of sovereign debt: A theory of cycles of populism and austerity (No. w21948). *National Bureau of Economic Research.*

Edwards, S. (2010). *Left behind: Latin America and the false promise of populism.* The University of Chicago Press.

Eichengreen, B. (2018). *The populist temptation: Economic grievance and political reaction in the modern era.* Oxford University Press.

Elliott, B. (2021). *The roots of populism: Neoliberalism and working-class lives.* Manchester University Press.

Funke, M., Schularick, M., & Trebesch, C. (2020). *Populist leaders and the economy* (CEPR Discussion Papers).

Galston, W. A. (2017). The 2016 US election: The populist moment. *Journal of Democracy, 28*(2), 21–33.

Harvey, D. (2007). *A brief history of neoliberalism.* Oxford University Press.

Hazony, Y. (2018). *The virtue of nationalism.* Basic Books.

Kaltwasser, C. R., Taggart, P., Ochoa Espejo, P., & Ostiguy, P. (2017). *The Oxford handbook of populism.* Oxford University Press.

Kenny, P. D. (2017). *Populism and patronage: Why populists win elections in India, Asia, and beyond.* Oxford University Press.

Krygier, M., Czarnota, A., & Sadurski, W. (Eds.). (2022). *Anti-constitutional populism.* Cambridge University Press.

Kyle, J., & Gultchin, L. (2018). *Populists in power around the world.* Tony Blair Institute.

Levitsky, S., & Ziblatt, D. (2018). *How democracies die.* Crown.

Mirowski, P., & Plehwe, D. (Eds.). (2009). *The road from Mont Pèlerin: The making of the neoliberal thought collective.* Harvard University Press.

Moffitt, B. (2016). *The global rise of populism: Performance, political style, and repression.* Stanford University Press.

Mudde, C. (2004). The populist zeitgeist. *Government and Opposition, 39*(3), 541–563.

Mudde, C. (2007). *Populist radical right parties in Europe.* Cambridge University Press.

Mudde, C., & Kaltwasser, C. R. (Eds.). (2012). *Populism in Europe and the Americas: Threat or corrective for democracy?* Cambridge University Press.

Mudde, C., & Kaltwasser, C. R. (2017). *Populism—A very short introduction.* Oxford University Press.

Müller, J. W. (2016). *What is populism?* University of Pennsylvania Press.

Norris, P. (2020). Measuring populism worldwide. *Party Politics, 26*(6), 697–717.

Ostiguy, P. (2017). Populism: A socio-cultural approach. In C. R. Kaltwasser, P. Taggart, P. Ochoa Espejo, & P. Ostiguy (Eds.), *The Oxford handbook of populism* (pp. 74–97). Oxford University Press.

Ostiguy, P., & Roberts, K. M. (2016). Putting Trump in comparative perspective: Populism and the politicization of the sociocultural low. *The Brown Journal of World Affairs, 23*(1), 25–50.

Prior, A., & van Hoef, Y. (2018). Interdisciplinary approaches to emotions in politics and international relations. *Politics and Governance, 6*(4), 48–52.

Rodrik, D. (2018). Populism and the economics of globalization. *Journal of International Business Policy, 1*(1), 12–33.

Taggart, P. (2000). *Populism.* Open University Press.

Urbinati, N. (2019). Me the people. In *Me the people.* Harvard University Press.

V-Dem Institute. (2022). *Defiance in the face of autocratization* (Democracy Report 2022). https://www.v-dem.net/documents/29/V-dem_democr acyreport2023_lowres.pdf

Weyland, K. (2013). Latin America's authoritarian drift: The threat from the populist left. *Journal of Democracy, 24*(3), 18–32.

Williamson, E. (1992). *The Penguin history of Latin America.* Penguin.

Zúquete, J. P. (2008). The missionary politics of Hugo Chávez Latin. *American Politics and Society, 5*(1), 91–121.

CHAPTER 3

A Threat to Liberty, Free Markets, and the Open Society

Abstract In this chapter the support for populist parties and regimes, and their threats to democracy, liberty, and the open society are summarized. It is shown how, over the last decades, populist voter support and the use of populist rhetoric have increased continuously, while democracy has been backsliding, and liberty, free markets, and the open society have been curtailed.

Keywords Threats to liberty and the open society · Populist voter support · Populist parties · Democratic backsliding · Illiberalism · Decline of economic freedom

It should be clear that populism, as I and most other scholars understand it, is a threat to liberty, free markets, and the open society. Even though it is not easy to measure the influence of populist parties and leaders due to the simple fact that populism, as shown above, is hard to strictly define and delimit, there can be no doubt about its popularity and consequences. During the last decades, populist voter support and the use of populist rhetoric have increased continuously, while democracy has been backsliding, and liberty, free markets, and the open society have been curtailed.

N. Karlson, *Reviving Classical Liberalism Against Populism*, Palgrave Studies in Classical Liberalism, https://doi.org/10.1007/978-3-031-49074-3_3

Populist Voter Support

According to e.g., the Timbro Authoritarian Populism Index from 2019 which primarily uses scholarly literature to categorize parties, the average voter support of populist parties with authoritarian tendencies in 2018 in European democracies was 22.2%. Populist parties were part of every third European government. The combined support for left- and right-wing populist parties equaled the support for social democratic parties and was twice the size of support for liberal parties (Heinö, 2019). The same is true in many other parts of the world (Freedom House, 2019).

Kyle and Gultchin (2018) identified 46 populist leaders or political parties globally that have held executive office across 33 countries between 1990 and 2018. They found that the number of populists in power around the world had increased fivefold, from four to 20. This included countries not only in Latin America and in Eastern and Central Europe—where populism has traditionally been most prevalent—but also in Asia and Western Europe. Whereas populism was once found primarily in emerging democracies, populists are increasingly gaining power in developed democracies.

Lührmann et al. (2020), based on an extensive expert survey, created a data set examining the policy positions and organizational structures of political parties between 1970 and 2019 across 169 countries around the world, generating a dataset on 1,955 political parties across 1,560 elections. The results show that the median governing party in democracies has become more illiberal in recent decades. This means that more parties show lower commitment to political pluralism, to problems with the demonization of political opponents, to respect for fundamental minority rights, and to problems with the encouragement of political violence. Some of these parties are new entrants, but a kind of populist drift also within established parties lies behind the result.

Based on a global expert survey covering 1052 parliamentary parties in 163 countries, Norris (2020) classified parties by their use of populist or pluralist rhetoric, including their use of the abovementioned 'us-versus-them' logic and whether they respect or undermine liberal democratic principles. 288 parties were classified as strongly populist. Almost half of these parties (104/288 or 46%) were estimated to be economically right-wing and socially conservative, but almost as many (95/288 or 42%) were socially conservative but located on the left toward the economy. Of the rest, only a few (20/288 or 9%) expressed socialist and social liberal values. Even fewer (9/288 or 4%) favored free markets and social liberal values.

DEMOCRATIC BACKSLIDING

While the studies referred to above are primarily based on the populist rhetorical style and discourse frames used, another indication of the success of populist policies can be traced through the backsliding of democracy and liberty that has occurred in recent years. As argued above, changing the institutional orientation of democracy towards authoritarianism is a core characteristic of populism, a logical consequence of populist strategies. Leading democracy scholar Larry Diamond (2020: 1) concludes that "a global democratic recession began in 2006 and has persisted – and deepened – over the past 14 years. Not only have average levels of freedom (or democratic quality) been declining globally and in most parts of the world, but the pace of democratic breakdown accelerated, and the number of democratic transitions declined, particularly in the past five years."

According to V-Dem Institute (2022), the level of democracy enjoyed by the average global citizen in 2022 is down to 1986 levels. Liberal democracies, with general elections *and* guaranteed civil and political rights, peaked in 2012 with 42 countries and are now down to the lowest levels in over 25 years—34 nations home to only 13% of the world's population (V-Dem Institute, 2021). The democratic decline is especially evident in Asia-Pacific, Eastern Europe, and Central Asia, as well as in parts of Latin America and the Caribbean. 72% of the world population— or 5.7 billion people—today lives in different sorts of autocracies. Just ten years ago it was only 46% (V-Dem Institute, 2022).

These results are confirmed by the latest edition of the Democracy Index from The Economist. It rates the state of democracy across 167 countries on the basis of five measures—electoral process and pluralism, the functioning of government, political participation, democratic political culture, and civil liberties—and finds that the global score fell from 5.37 to a new low of 5.28 out of ten in 2021. This means that more than a third of the world's population live under authoritarian rule while just 6.4% enjoy a full democracy (Economist, 2022). Also, an index like Transparency International's Corruption Perceptions Index (2021) shows that the global average remains unchanged for the tenth year in a row, at just 43 out of a possible 100 points.

A Worldwide Illiberal Turn

All this does not mean that general elections have disappeared or that markets have been substituted by planned economies. Instead, what has happened is that liberal institutions fundamental to both markets and democracies, as well as civil society—the rule of law, independent courts, freedom of expression, and other civic and political liberties—have been weakened or started to crumble.

A free and open society requires, as Karl Popper, Friedrich Hayek, Milton Friedman, Robert Dahl and many others have argued, that individual economic, civil, and political liberties are upheld, private property rights are safe, the press and media are free, the courts are independent, minorities have rights, and the democracy is constitutionally bound. A free society is a pluralistic society, not a plebiscitarian, clan society where a self-proclaimed majority has authoritarian powers.

However, according to the Human Freedom Index (2021) 83% of the global population lives in jurisdictions that have seen a fall in human freedom since 2008. That includes decreases in overall freedom in the 10 most populous countries in the world. Only 17% of the global population lives in countries that have seen increases in freedom over the same time.

Also, the pace of economic liberalization has slowed in the 2000s, compared to advances in the 1980s and 1990s, even though it continues in most countries. According to the index of economic freedom, which measures economic freedom in five dimensions (Fraser, 2021), the average economic freedom rating increased to 7.04 from 6.61 points between 2000 and 2019. However, since historic improvements in the legal structure and property rights have been the main force behind long-term gains in economic liberty (Prados de la Escosura, 2016), there are reasons to believe that the rise of populism in the coming years will have negative consequences in this regard too. In fact, according to the most recent index, which includes the Covid-19 pandemic, there was a sharp decrease in economic freedom in 2021 (Fraser, 2022).

All these threats to liberty and the open society cannot, of course, be blamed on populism alone—there are other kinds of authoritarian regimes such as China, Russia, North Korea, Cuba, Vietnam, and Myanmar as well. But at least in the developed Western democracies of the world, populism is arguably a major reason.

REFERENCES

Diamond, L. (2020). Democratic regression in comparative perspective: Scope, methods, and causes. *Democratization*, 1–21.

Economist. (2022). *A new low for global democracy. More pandemic restrictions damaged democratic freedoms in 2021.* https://www.economist.com/graphic-detail/2022/02/09/a-new-low-for-global-democracy?utm_content=article-link-1&etear=nl_today_1&utm_campaign=a.the-economist-today&utm_medium=email.internal-newsletter.np&utm_source=salesforce-marketing-cloud&utm_term=2/9/2022&utm_id=1045717

Fraser. (2021). *Economic freedom of the world: 2019 annual report.* Fraser Institute.

Fraser. (2022). *Economic freedom of the world: 2022 annual report.* Fraser Institute.

Freedom House. (2019). *Democracy in retreat. Freedom in the world 2019.* Freedom House. https://ourworldindata.org/democracy. Gathered January 13, 2023.

Heinö, A. (2019). *Timbro Authoritarian Populism Index 2019.* https://populismindex.com/report/. Gathered January 13, 2023.

Human Freedom Index. (2021). Cato Institute. https://www.cato.org/human-freedom-index/2021

Kyle, J., & Gultchin, L. (2018). *Populists in power around the world.* Tony Blair Institute.

Lührmann, L. Medzihorsky, J., Hindle, G., & Lindberg, S. I. (2020). *New global data on political parties: V-Party* (Briefing paper No. 9). V-Dem Institute. https://www.v-dem.net/static/website/img/refs/vparty_briefing.pdf

Prados de la Escosura, L. (2016). Economic freedom in the long run: Evidence from OECD countries (1850–2007). *Economic History Review, 69*(2), 435–468.

Norris, P. (2020). Measuring populism worldwide. *Party Politics, 26*(6), 697–717.

Transparency International's Corruption Perceptions Index. (2021). *Corruption Perception Index.* https://www.transparency.org/en/cpi/2021

V-Dem Institute. (2021). *Autocratization turns viral* (Democracy Report 2021). https://www.v-dem.net/static/website/files/dr/dr_2021.pdf

V-Dem Institute. (2022). *Defiance in the face of autocratization* (Democracy Report 2022). https://www.v-dem.net/documents/29/V-dem_democracyreport2023_lowres.pdf

Open Access This chapter is licensed under the terms of the Creative Commons Attribution 4.0 International License (http://creativecommons.org/licenses/by/4.0/), which permits use, sharing, adaptation, distribution and reproduction in any medium or format, as long as you give appropriate credit to the original author(s) and the source, provide a link to the Creative Commons license and indicate if changes were made.

The images or other third party material in this chapter are included in the chapter's Creative Commons license, unless indicated otherwise in a credit line to the material. If material is not included in the chapter's Creative Commons license and your intended use is not permitted by statutory regulation or exceeds the permitted use, you will need to obtain permission directly from the copyright holder.

CHAPTER 4

Explaining Populism and Autocratization

Abstract In this chapter the most popular explanations that have been proposed for why and how populists succeed are discussed and synthesized into "a populist model of autocratization". Explanations dealing with (1) globalization, immigration, and policy failures; (2) culture and identity; (3) psychology and human nature; (4) social media and echo chambers; and (5) charismatic leaders and policy entrepreneurs, are included in the analysis. My conclusion is that the populist ideas, beliefs, and values, related to identity and shaped by the populist rhetorical style and discourse frames, play the central role.

Keywords Explaining populism · Autocratic change · Autocratization · Globalization · Immigration · Culture · Identity · Psychology · Human nature · Social media · Charismatic leaders

How can we understand the rise of populism? Why do so many people support the rhetorical style and institutional orientation that populists employ? How do populists promote their autocratic ambitions? These are of course *the* questions to answer for those who favor liberty, liberal democracy, and the open society.

One answer could be the populist political strategies themselves, presented in Chapter 2 above. That the populist rhetoric and framing

N. Karlson, *Reviving Classical Liberalism Against Populism*,
Palgrave Studies in Classical Liberalism,
https://doi.org/10.1007/978-3-031-49074-3_4

to achieve polarization and the creeping autocratization in themselves are sufficient to explain the rise of populism described in the last chapter. There is truth to this, but as we shall see it is not what previous research emphasizes. Also, there is a need to understand *why* populist rhetoric and framing tend to be so effective. In this chapter, some of the most popular explanations in existing research will therefore be presented. These explanations are highly interdisciplinary, drawing on theories and results from many disciplines.

ANALYZING POPULISM AS AUTOCRATIC INSTITUTIONAL CHANGE

In a previous book, *Statecraft and Liberal Reforms in Advanced Democracies* (Karlson, 2018), I developed a general theory for how institutional change can be explained and promoted. The theory was based on a synthesis of previous research about institutional change and an extended comparative case study of liberal reforms in Sweden and Australia over the last 30 years. The democratic backsliding and weakening of the open society described in the last chapter are all examples of institutional or policy changes and could thus be analyzed by a similar framework, albeit with changes in a non-liberal direction. This is the approach taken here to structure the analysis.

According to this theory, the process of institutional change starts with changing economic and social conditions that affect voters and other economic and social actors. It could be changes in technologies or trade patterns that affect the jobs and income prospects of different groups in society, or failures of welfare or educational policies, just to mention a few possibilities. These in turn create a demand for new policy ideas for how to handle the consequences of the changing conditions. Such ideas need to be articulated and acted upon by different policy entrepreneurs that interact with and activate power resources and interests, which influence changes in institutions and policies. Next, these changes affect the social and economic conditions of voters, and the cycle of institutional changes continues. I called this "the reform circle".

Ideas, or in other words beliefs and values, play a key role in the theory. The ability of different policy entrepreneurs to use idea-based strategies to frame or condition how different interests interpret or understand the changing economic and social conditions, as well as the existing institutions and policies, is decisive for how and in what direction institutions change.

More generally, ideas in terms of beliefs and values matter for how economic and social changes are interpreted. Ideas condition how people and different interests interpret or understand the economic and social conditions, as well as the existing institutions and policies, of their society (Karlson, 2018). As argued by Blyth (2002), ideas serve to reduce uncertainty, facilitate collective action, coalition building, and coordination, and are used as weapons for transforming existing institutions. McCloskey (1985) and Majone (1992), among others, point out the importance of rhetoric in arguing for institutional change. Ideas thus can explain why people-facing the same economic circumstances—still make different choices. Interests and power resources are so to speak ideationally bound.

Notice also that party politics or tactics in the narrower sense has a more limited role in the model. While even different Machiavellian strategies may be decisive to build coalitions and push reforms through parliament, the overall direction of the process of institutional change has other explanations.

In the coming sections, some of the most popular, but partial, explanations of populism in previous research will be synthesized in a similar model to the one presented above. In Fig. 4.1 this populist model of autocratization is presented.

Starting from the left, existing institutions and policies in period 1 cause policy failures or are insufficient to handle changing economic and social conditions, perhaps even creating a crisis of some sort. Or the existing conditions may just become interpreted differently through the framing of populist ideas, beliefs, and values. These economic and social conditions in turn influence not only the interests of different groups or

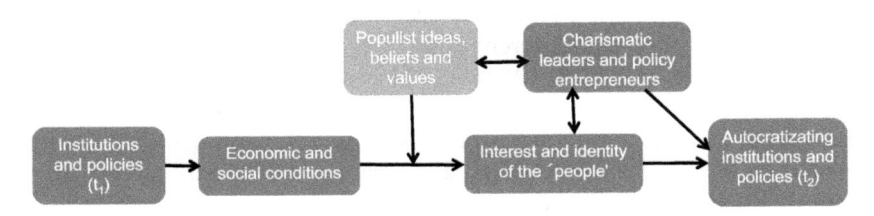

Fig. 4.1 The populist model of autocratization

the population at large, but also their cultural and social identities, which affect the 'people' or voter majority, and thus the power resources necessary to change the institutions and policies in period 2 in an autocratic direction. How the voters interpret how such changes in economic and social conditions influence their interests and identities is largely shaped by their ideas, beliefs, and values.

The institutions and policies in period 2, perhaps initially with just small autocratic tendencies, will in turn affect the economic and social conditions, which will affect the interest and identity of the 'people', interpreted through the populist ideas, beliefs, and values, that change the institutions in period 3. By this time the populist leaders and their policy entrepreneurs may also have a direct influence on the institutions and policies. And so on, the process continues into something that perhaps may be called a *cycle of autocratization*, quite like the twelve-step program presented in Chapter 2.

Globalization, Immigration, and Policy Failures

The most popular explanation for the rise of populism is that different policy failures have caused a deterioration of the economic and social conditions for important groups and voters in our societies. The argument is that these failures and the austerity policy measures taken to handle them have then been exploited by populist parties and policy entrepreneurs.

To argue that changing economic conditions is a cause behind institutional change is a standard way of thinking among economists that goes back to Marx (1867), later followed by prominent scholars of institutional change like North (1981, 1990), Buchanan (1986) and Acemoglu et al. (2005). The common argument used in the case of populism is that globalization, automation, and neoliberal policies have deteriorated the economic and social conditions causing unemployment, insecurity, austerity, inequality, and different crises.

One example is Rodrik (2018, 2021), who argues that the rise of populism is rooted in a desire to reclaim popular democracy and national autonomy, against economic problems caused by international trade, in particular imports from China, and financial globalization. Similarly, Mounk (2018) and Eichengreen (2018) argue that a major factor behind the rise of populism is various economic problems affecting ordinary voters, and consequently see "fixing the economy" as a primary remedy against populism.

Over the last two or three decades the welfare states of the Western world have indeed started to crumble due to internal contradictions, rent seeking, and deficits (Karlson, 2019). Due to Baumol's law, the low productivity of many tax-funded services has led to a structural increase in the costs of public welfare that probably is not long-run sustainable (Baumol, 1993; Mahon, 2007). Therefore, in many Western democracies, there is growing discontent with the quality of the publicly provided welfare services, but also with the quality of core state activities such as public order and defense. Even though many voters still are favorably disposed to the welfare state's goals and ambitions, they simultaneously are critical of its policy outcomes (Lindell & Pelling, 2021; Roosma et al., 2013).

For example, socio-economic groups that earlier voted for the social democratic parties form the basis of the support of some far-right parties (Mudde, 2017). These voters may well long for the return of the traditional welfare state and believe that its benefits are threatened by globalization and immigration.

Similarly rising inequality is often blamed for causing populism. Several scholars (e. g. Milanovic, 2016; Norris & Inglehart, 2019; O'Connor, 2017) have argued that economic inequality is a core factor behind the rise of populism. The arguments are similar to those of Piketty (2014), arguing that financial capitalism causes recurring crises and a higher rate of return on capital than on labor.

Sometimes these kinds of arguments are put in ideational or ideological terms, mirroring the left-wing populist rhetoric style presented in Chapter 2, blaming "neoliberalism". Hence, deregulations, privatizations, cuts in welfare programs, and free markets are accused of creating imbalances that are said to explain why populism emerges (Cayla, 2021; Kelly & Pike, 2017). It is interesting to note how also leading political scientists like Sheri Berman (2021) and Francis Fukuyama (2022) have adopted this style of argumentation. Especially, Latin American populism is often said to have been caused by "neoliberalism" (Roberts, 1995; Edwards, 2022; Weyland, 1996). On the right, similar kinds of arguments are echoed by Patrick Deneen (2018), Yoram Hazony (2018), and others who claim that liberalism and free markets have depleted the moral and social foundations of our societies.

Nevertheless, it is true that international trade and automation always have both winners and losers—perhaps especially low-skilled workers in manufacturing industries in developed countries (Lakner & Milanovic, 2013). For example, Colantone and Stanig (2018) showed that Chinese import shocks strengthened the support for nationalist and isolationist parties in some Western European countries. Dippel et al. (2015) found that voting for extreme-right parties respond significantly to trade integration with China and Eastern Europe in Germany from 1987 to 2009. Other country-level and subnational European studies give similar results (Guriev & Papaioannou, 2022). Similarly, Autor et al. (2021) showed that US congressional districts exposed to increases in import penetration removed moderate representatives from office and replaced them with more extreme candidates.

But structural and technological changes and economic restructuring caused by free trade, capitalism, and market processes are not something new. The same things have happened again and again during the last decades and even centuries. And as Schumpeter (1942 [1994]), Baumol (2002), and many others have shown these processes are at the same time the perhaps most important factors behind economic growth, increasing real wages, welfare, and prosperity for the majority of voters. The same processes have simultaneously contributed to improved health, increased life spans, lower child death rates, etc. for everyone. This is the overall experience of the last centuries in both East and West. There is substantial empirical evidence supporting this (see e.g. Friedman, 2017; North, 1981, 1990, 1994; McCloskey 2006; Rosenberg & Birdzell, 1987). Hence, while this cannot be the major explanation behind the rise of populism, it may well be a decisive factor for groups that are negatively affected.

A problem with these kinds of explanations is also why countries like Austria and France, or the Scandinavian countries with low and almost stable levels of income inequality, massive redistribution, and extensive welfare programs still are affected by populism. It is also puzzling that changes like these would cause rightwing (and not left-wing) populism, which as we have seen is the typical kind of populism in developed countries. Moreover, in many countries like India, Israel, and Poland the large majority of the population has benefitted substantially from globalization, and yet they have all recently elected populist governments.

The same is true concerning the effects of economic or financial crises, causing rising unemployment and usually fiscal austerity. While the recession in 2008–2009, just like the Euro crisis that followed in several southern European countries, provided fertile ground for populist rhetoric and leaders, it was rightwing populist parties that gained the most, not their leftwing adversaries (Guriev & Papaioannou, 2022).

Bergh and Kärnä (2021), based on the vote shares for 267 right-wing and left-wing populist parties in 33 European countries during 1980–2017, and globalization data from the KOF institute, found no evidence of a positive association between (economic or other types of) globalization and populism. Most controls were insignificant, including the Gini index in inequality of disposal income. Interestingly, the share of immigrants was significantly *negatively* related to the vote shares of populists.

Immigration is otherwise another popular argument behind the rise of populism (e.g., Borjas, 2014; Dustmann et al., 2005). Some argue that immigrants take away jobs from native workers and suppress their wages. Others say that immigrants do not work and rely on the host country's generous welfare system. Many claims that immigrants' values and social norms are incompatible with those of the host country, posing an existential threat to its identity and culture.

However, according to Guriev and Papaioannou (2022), the actual evidence is mixed. A first problem is that the public perceptions of the size of immigration differ considerably from the reality—according to Alesina et al. (2018) the *perceived* levels of immigrant stocks are two to three times higher than actual levels in countries like France, Germany, Italy, Sweden, and the US. Moreover, both in the UK and Austria local levels of EU immigration and refugee assignment, respectively, actually lowered the leave vote in the EU referendum and the support for the Austrian populist party FPÖ (Colantone & Stanig, 2018; Steinmayr, 2021). It is also important to observe that the number of immigrants and refugees is very low in countries like Hungary and Poland, which still have populist governments.

So, while failing policies may indeed have contributed to different social and economic problems, especially for some groups, it is hard to see that this is the major explanation. In general, there seems to be a strong bias in large parts of the populist literature to take the economic and social developments in the US, and perhaps the UK, where median wages have stagnated and income distribution worsened over the last three decades, as a being representative to all countries (Velasco, 2020). Margalit (2019), after surveying the relevant literature, concludes that the overall explanatory evidence of the kind of economic arguments presented above for the support of populism is modest: at the most, they can explain the outcome on the margin. Perhaps we may say that changing economic and social conditions sometimes may serve as *enabling conditions* for populism.

But let us also briefly mention a seemingly different set of institutional failures concerning democracy itself. For example, Grzymala-Busse (2019) argues that populism is arising from the failures of elite competition in democracies. The mainstream parties are said to fail to respond to popular grievances, demonstrate accountability, and offer credible political alternatives, and instead collude on economic issues, conceding both rents and sovereignty to governing elites and supra-national organizations such as the European Union.

However, this is almost identical to the arguments discussed above about economic policy failures and the purported "neoliberal" policy responses. It may well be that many democracies have underperformed compared to some indicators and that some policies have contributed to different social and economic problems, but as argued above it is hard to see this as the major cause behind populism. Most democracies have experienced problems with misguided policies before, as in the 1970s, without having these kinds of consequences.

A more important democratic problem and institutional failure, however, may be the connection between corruption and populism. As we saw in Chapter 2, populists often accuse elites and established parties of being corrupt. In many cases, populists also use this as an excuse to dismantle democratic institutions (Mudde & Kaltwasser, 2012). If corruption really is prevalent, as it turned out to be in Italy in the early 1990s for example, then this will benefit populist parties. There seems to be substantial empirical evidence for this in Eastern Europe (Kossow, 2019). What is questionable, however, is how effective populist leaders are in actually fighting corruption. I shall return to the question of the rule of law in Chapter 6.

This brings us over to non-economic explanations. Structural changes like those presented above need to be interpreted and understood as good or bad, as just or unjust, as beneficial, or not, to have a causal effect. And there is a need for some kind of agency to make this happen.

Culture and Identity

Non-economic arguments are often put under the heading of a cultural backlash. For example, based om extensive survey data, Norris and Inglehart (2019) argue that populism is the result of a conservative backlash and authoritarian reflex due to, basically, increasing social divisions, rising inequality, worsening economic conditions for large groups of voters, especially of an older generation in rural areas. Similarly, Rodrik (2021), argues that "culture, racial attitudes, and social identity" provide a causal pathway through which globalization shocks and economic dislocation influence support for populist parties and candidates.

The causal relationship may, however, just as well run in the opposite direction: namely, in the sense that cultural concerns and grievances shape people's beliefs about economic change and its adverse impact on their standing (Margalit, 2019). People who worry about cultural homogeneity or changing cultural aspects of identity and community may be more likely to adopt the views that, for example, immigration and multiculturalism are having negative economic consequences. Immigration may thus cause both economic and cultural anxiety. There is considerable evidence consistent with this view (Brader et al., 2008; Sniderman & Hagendoorn, 2007).

An illustrative example is the book *What's the Matter with Kansas? How Conservatives Won the Heart of America* by journalist and historian Frank (2004), who explores the support for anti-elitist conservative policies in Kansas, which he argues were against the economic interests of the majority of the voters in the state. By shifting the political discourse from social and economic equality to cultural issues, such as abortion and gay marriage, voters' interest was redirected to fuel anger toward the "liberal elites". Similarly, referred to by Rodrik (2021), Hacker and Pierson (2020) argue that this is exactly the strategy the Republican Party has pursued to advance a right-wing policy agenda—tax reduction, deregulation, weakening of labor market protections, and cuts in social insurance—that benefited the wealthy. While all this, of course, can be debated, it nevertheless shows that culture in terms of ideas, beliefs, and values often matters more than economic interests. Identity trumps interests, a fact that may be hard to accept for some economists.

There is some empirical support for these views. In a study, combining surveys and experiments, in Poland, the UK, and the US, Marchlewska et al. (2018) found that perceived ingroup disadvantage and collective narcissism—the conviction that they have a superior vision of what it means to be a true citizen of their nation—led to support for populism. Noury and Roland (2020) in a review of the literature on the rise of identity politics and populism in Europe found a complex interaction between economic and cultural factors. They argue that economic anxiety among large groups of voters related to the financial crises in 2008–2009 and the austerity policies that followed triggered a heightened receptivity to the messages of cultural backlash from populist parties.

Still, culture is a loose concept that can mean many different things. From an ethnographic point of view (LeVine, 1984), culture represents a shared consensus on meanings among members of an interacting community, similar to the consensus on language, grammar, and pronunciation among members of a speech community. It is collective but is learned, consciously or unconsciously, through individual interaction with others. Similarly, D'Andrade (1984: 116) sees "culture as consisting of learned systems of meaning, communicated by means of natural language and other symbol systems, having representational, directive, and affective functions, and capable of creating cultural entities and particular senses of reality. Through these systems of meaning, groups of people adapt to their environment and structure interpersonal activities."

Importantly, culture can change. For example, Putnam (2020), using numerous data sources and surveys shows that in the US the overall culture has become more individualistic and self-centered since the 1960s, moving from "We to I", as he says, with lower social trust, bipartisanship, civic do-gooding, and community, in their view resulting in populist policies and uncompromising" hyper-partisanship".

But again, it is hard to see that culture itself can be the major explanation behind populism. Culture, in terms of norms, traditions, and customs, only changes slowly, much more slowly than the economy and most formal institutions (Williamson, 2000). Hence, it is hard to see that the rise of populism over the last couple of decades can be explained by culture alone. At the same time, it should be obvious that at least right-wing populists often advance threats to cultural identity as a way to promote their institutional objectives. How changes in economic and social changes affect the cultural identity of people may be just as important as the effects on their economic interests. And as we shall see in the next chapter, this is also largely true for left-wing populists.

Psychology and Human Nature

Another type of non-economic, non-rational explanation behind the rise of populism has to do with psychology and human nature. Already in the classic book *Escape from Freedom* (1941), Erich Fromm argued that it was psychological conditions that could provide the explanation for the rise of authoritarianism in the 1930s. Modern research in social and moral psychology largely confirms such a view.

To start, there is broad support for the view that humans have a "duplex mind" (Baumeister, 2005), that the mind operates on at least two levels, where one is more intuitive and automatic, while the other is rational and conscious. Kahneman (2011) called these System 1 and System 2 respectively, arguing that intuitive decisions are fast, automatic, and effortless, while rational decisions are slower and are taken in a serial, effortful, and more controlled fashion. Often the former, more intuitive systems take over, making us use different simplifying heuristics, instead of rational reasoning, which causes different kinds of biases in our decisions. This is where the lure of populism may come in.

According to Feldman and Stenner (1997) human nature is characterized by an authoritarian predisposition, a deep-seated, relatively enduring psychological predisposition to prefer—indeed, to demand—obedience and conformity, over tolerance, freedom, and diversity. This predisposition, she argues, is latent, but may be triggered.

Moral psychologist Jonathan Haidt, in *The Righteous Mind: Why Good People Are Divided by Politics and Religion* (2012), similarly argues that our minds are designed for the populist, groupish righteousness, that our behavior and ways of thinking are largely based on neurological intuitions that drive our strategic, rationalistic reasoning. Hence, we are intrinsically moralistic, critical, and judgmental fostering polarization between groups and society at large. In other words, humans have a *tribal mind* that can be activated by populist rhetoric and leaders. In a somewhat similar way Anne Applebaum argues in her best-selling book *Twilight of Democracy: The Seductive Lure of Authoritarianism* (2020) that political systems with simple, populistic beliefs are inherently appealing, that there is a "seductive lure of authoritarianism".

Boudry and Hofhuis (2018) even argue that cultural evolution, under certain circumstances, may develop "parasites of mind", systems of misbelief that subvert the interests of their human hosts. An example could be the historical belief in witchcraft, but the argument may be equally applicable to populist ideas and modern conspiracy theories like QAnon. Such systems of belief may become self-validating and exhibit a surprising degree of resilience in the face of adverse evidence and criticism (Boudry & Braeckman, 2012).

Social Media and Echo Chambers

Such parasites or lures may have become particularly important due to the growth of digital social media in recent decades. There is a growing amount of research that shows that social media is a key factor behind the rise of populism.

Initially, this new technology was seen as creating new sources of information that would strengthen democracy and participation. As Gurri (2018), argued, social media mobilized millions of ordinary people around the world, clearing the ground for the Arab Spring and viable critiques of institutional failures in many countries. The new information technologies enabled the public to break the power of the political hierarchies and experts. Traditional gatekeepers were weakened, and once marginal movements and politicians became empowered. In this way, digital media was a force of freedom and democracy.

However, over time digitalization and social media seem to have led to polarization and the denigration of independent journalists, to the expense of open, evidence-based public debate (Mounk, 2018). In an impressive survey of the current literature Tumber and Waisbord (2021) show that recent transformations in digital social media are highly conducive to the kind of polarized, anti-rational, post-fact, post-truth communication championed by populism. Digital platform tools have, using algorithms, making it possible, as part of their successful business models, to amplify content to segments of the population, often for political purposes, creating a powerful, unaccountable, and often untraceable method of targeting misinformation and conspiracy theories.

Hence, deliberate polarization and misinformation by populist activists and leaders have created filter bubbles and echo chambers where algorithms dictate what we encounter online, where users are exposed to views and opinions they already agree with while being sheltered from opposing perspectives (Sumpter, 2018). These echo chambers hamper balanced decision-making and undermine public discourse, and thus the foundations of democracy itself. Moreover, populist political leaders increasing, as was argued in Chapter 2, deliberately try to control both public and private media to create polarization and boost support (Shayegh et al., 2021). As shown by Tumber and Waisbord (2021), the control of social media for such purposes has become prevalent on all continents. Using the tower of Babel as a metaphor, Haidt (2022) argues that social media has led to stupidity and the fragmentation of everything:

> Facebook, Twitter, YouTube, and a few other large platforms unwittingly dissolved the mortar of trust, and belief in institutions, and shared stories that had held a large and diverse secular democracy together.

CHARISMATIC LEADERS AND POLICY ENTREPRENEURS

An additional important explanation behind the rise of populism that has been proposed concerns the role of the leaders, or in terms of the explanatory model above: the policy entrepreneurs. They are the main actors that develop, articulate, and communicate new ideas, facts, perspectives, values, and worldviews to activate power resources and interests, and to Influence public opinion and other decision-makers (Baumgartner & Jones, 1993; Karlson, 2018; Kingdon, 1984; López & Leighton, 2013; Mintrom, 1997). Without agency, no change.

According to Weyland (2017, 2022), personalistic charismatic leadership, usually sustained by direct connections to an unorganized mass of followers, is central to populism. Typical examples are Alberto Fujimori and Hugo Chávez in Latin America, Viktor Orbán and Recep Tayyip Erdoğan in Europe, Rodrigo Duterte and Narendra Modi in Asia, and Donald Trump in the US.

Such leaders, as we have seen in Chapter 2, seek to establish a direct relationship with the people, circumventing parliaments, and often party structures, through mass meetings, television performances, or social media. They are experts in using the populist rhetorical style and discursive framing to gain power and promote institutional change in their desired direction. The 'us-versus-them' logic, calling for the recognition of ordinary people, and narratives about corrupt elites, 'others' that threatens the identity of true people, and emotional arguments about meaning and community are used systematically.

Populist leaders often see themselves as symbols, embodying the true people. For example., Alberto Fujimori in Peru in 1990 crafted his campaign with the nonelite slogan "A President Like You" (Levitsky &

Loxton, 2013: 167). Similarly, former Venezuelan President Hugo Chávez, used "Chávez is the people!" as a slogan. But, as pointed out in Chapter 2, a special challenge is to balance such ordinariness with extraordinariness (Moffitt, 2016). How can you both be just like the people and at the same time be so talented and special as to rise above the people and be their leader and representative? Various techniques are used to show such extraordinariness, including showing off wealth, and masculinity, and presenting themselves as the singular figure who can fix the economy, law and order, etc. Just think of leaders like Rodrigo Duterte in the Philippines, Silvio Berlusconi in Italy, or Donald Trump in the US.

Surprisingly little, however, has been done about how other policy entrepreneurs support or interact with populist leaders. It is likely that different special interests groups form themselves into "policy coalitions" to influence the specific policies promoted by the populist regime (Sabatier & Weible, 2007; Sabatier & Zafonte, 2001). It is not hard to think of different groups, even if they may not fully support the populist ideas, that have an interest in tax cuts, redistribution, limiting immigration, supporting protectionist measures or in extending welfare benefits, or getting subsidies or protection for certain industries, not to say of becoming plutocrats themselves. In Latin America, an obvious example of such "policy entrepreneurs" are groups within the military (Scharpf, 2020), while in Eastern Europe oligarchs are the likely candidates (Carpenter, 2020). In all democracies, as Mancur Olson (1965, 1982) and many others have shown, there are special interests will free ride on the common good.

Explaining Populist Institutional Change

All the above-mentioned factors clearly have a role in explaining why populism is popular and how populist institutional change comes about.

Changing economic and social conditions, such as globalization, failing welfare programs, crises, inequality, and immigration may certainly provide fertile ground for populists to promote their ideas. And especially so if they are framed in ideological terms. But by themselves, these kinds of changing conditions are insufficient to explain populism. Instead, cultural factors about identity need to be taken into account. Also, humans seem to have a latent authoritarian predisposition, that our minds are psychologically designed for populist tribalism and righteousness, fostering polarization between groups and in society at large. Moreover, digital social media is highly conducive to the kind of polarized, anti-rational, post-fact, post-truth communication championed by populists. Algorithms and platform tools have created methods for targeting misinformation and conspiracy theories to large audiences creating echo chambers where populist beliefs are sustained.

This is where the real importance of populism comes in: populist leaders deliberately use ideas, beliefs, and values—the populist rhetoric and discursive framing—to shape or condition these interpretations. Human nature and the active use of social media help in this endeavor. The populist leaders also directly influence the voter majority and other interests that hold the power resources needed to promote their populist institutional orientation of autocratization. Left- and right-wing populists, as presented in Chapter 2, may even form a symbiotic relationship in this process, each promoting the polarization of society, in a self-enforcing process.

Populist ideas, beliefs, and values, and in particular those relating to identity, shaped by the distinct rhetorical style and discourse frames, play the central role in this process of autocratization as presented in Fig. 4.1. While ideological and cultural factors about identity and the like can be seen as ideas in terms of values and beliefs, the same is hardly true for humans' latent authoritarian predispositions or tribal minds. Neither are the digital social media that are used to promote populist polarization. But fake news certainly can. What we may say, however, is that all these factors may enhance the effects of populist ideas in certain circumstances.

In the next chapter, we shall further explore the populist ideas, values, and beliefs, what I shall call, *populist collectivistic identity politics*.

REFERENCES

Acemoglu, D., Johnson, S., & Robinson, J. A. (2005). Institutions as a fundamental cause of long-run growth. *Handbook of Economic Growth, 1*(A), 385–472.

Alesina, A., Miano, A., & Stantcheva, S. (2018). *Immigration and redistribution* (No. w24733). National Bureau of Economic Research.

Applebaum, A. (2020). *Twilight of democracy: The seductive lure of authoritarianism*. Anchor.

Autor, D., Dorn, D., & Hanson, G. H. (2021). *On the persistence of the China shock* (No. w29401). National Bureau of Economic Research.

Baumeister, R. F. (2005). *The cultural animal: Human nature, meaning, and social life*. Oxford University Press.

Baumgartner, F., & Jones, B. (1993). *Agendas and instability in American politics*. University of Chicago Press.

Baumol, W. (1993). Health care, education and the cost disease: A looming crisis for public choice. *Public Choice, 77*(1), 17–28.

Baumol, W. (2002). *The free-market innovation machine: Analyzing the growth miracle of capitalism*. Princeton University Press.

Bergh, A., & Kärnå, A. (2021). Globalization and populism in Europe. *Public Choice, 189*(5–6), 1–20.

Berman, S. (2021). The Causes of Populism in the West. *Annual Review of Political Science, 24*, 71–88.

Blyth, M. (2002). *Great transformations*. Cambridge University Press.

Borjas, G. J. (2014). *Immigration economics*. Harvard University Press.

Boudry, M., & Braeckman, J. (2012). How convenient! The epistemic rationale of self-validating belief systems. *Philosophical Psychology, 25*(3), 341–364.

Boudry, M., & Hofhuis, S. (2018). Parasites of the mind. Why cultural theorists need the meme's eye view. *Cognitive System Research, 52*, 155–167.

Brader, T., Valentino, N., & Suhay, E. (2008). Is it immigration or the immigrants? The emotional influence of groups on public opinion and political action. *American Journal of Political Science, 52*(4), 959–978.

Buchanan, J. (1986). The constitution of economic policy. *American Economic Review, 77*(3), 243–250.

Carpenter, M. (2020). *The Europe whole and free: Europe's struggle against illiberal oligarchy*. The Polish Institute of International Affairs, PISM. https://pism.pl/publications/The_Europe_Whole_And_Free_Europes_Struggle_Against_Illiberal_Oligarchy. Gathered January 13, 2023.

Cayla, D. (2021). *Populism and neoliberalism*. Routledge.

Colantone, I., & Stanig, P. (2018). Global competition and Brexit. *American Political Science Review, 112*(2), 201–218.

D'Andrade, R. G. (1984). Cultural meaning systems. In R. A. Shweder & R. A. LeVine (Eds.), *Culture theory. Essays on mind, self and emotion* (pp. 88–119). Cambridge University Press.

Deneen, P. (2018). *Why liberalism failed*. Yale University Press.

Dippel, C., Gold, R., & Heblich, S. (2015). *Globalization and its (dis-)content: Trade shocks and voting behaviour* (NBER Working Paper No. 21812).

Dustmann, C., Fabbri, F., & Preston, I. (2005). The impact of immigration on the British labour market. *The Economic Journal, 115*(507), F324–F341.

Eichengreen, B. (2018). *The populist temptation: Economic grievance and political reaction in the modern era*. Oxford University Press.

Feldman, S., & Stenner, K. (1997). Perceived threat and authoritarianism. *Political Psychology, 18*(4), 741–770.

Frank, T. (2004). *What's the matter with Kansas*. Metropolitan Books.

Friedman, B. M. (2017). The moral consequences of economic growth. In *Markets, morals & religion* (pp. 29–42). Routledge.

Fromm, E. (1941). *The escape from freedom*. Farrar & Rinehart.

Fukuyama, F. (2022). *Liberalism and its discontents*. Profile Books.

Grzymala-Busse, A. (2019). Conclusion: The global forces of populism. *Polity, 51*(4), 718–723.

Guriev, S., & Papaioannou, E. (2022). The political economy of populism. *Journal of Economic Literature, 60*(3), 753–832.

Gurri, M. (2018). *The revolt of the public and the crisis of authority in the new millennium*. Stripe Press.

Hacker, J. S., & Pierson, P. (2020). *Let them eat tweets: How the right rules in an age of extreme inequality*. Liveright.

Haidt, J. (2012). *The righteous mind: Why good people are divided by politics and religion*. Vintage.

Haidt, J. (2022). Why the past 10 years of American life have been uniquely stupid. *The Atlantic, 11*. https://www.theatlantic.com/magazine/archive/2022/05/social-media-democracy-trust-babel/629369/

Hazony, Y. (2018). *The virtue of nationalism*. Basic Books.

Kahneman, D. (2011). *Thinking, fast and slow* (1st ed.). Farrar, Straus and Giroux.

Karlson, N. (2018). *Statecraft and liberal reform in advanced democracies*. Palgrave Macmillan.

Karlson, N. (2019). The idea Vacuum of liberalism and the quest for meaning and community. *Journal of Contextual Economics—Schmollers Jahrbuch, 139*(2–4), 259–269.

Kelly, P., & Pike, J. (Eds.). (2017). *Neo-liberalism and austerity: The moral economies of young people's health and well-being*. Palgrave Macmillan.

Kingdon, J. W. (1984). *Agendas, alternatives, and public policies*. Little Brown.

Kossow, N. (2019). *Populism and corruption*. Transparency International. https://knowledgehub.transparency.org/assets/uploads/helpdesk/populism-and-corruption-2019-final.pdf

Lakner, C., & Milanovic, B. (2013). *Global income distribution: From the fall of the Berlin wall to the great recession*.(Policy Research Working Paper, No. 6719). World Bank, Washington, DC.

LeVine, R. (1984). Property of culture: An ethnographic view. In R. A. Shweder & R. A. LeVine (Eds.), *Culture theory. Essays on mind, self and emotion* (pp. 67–87). Cambridge University Press.

Levitsky, S., & Loxton, J. (2013). Populism and competitive authoritarianism in the Andes. *Democratization, 20*(1), 107–136.

Lindell, J., & Pelling, L. (2021). *Det svenska missnöjet*. Atlas.

López, E., & Leighton, W. (2013). *Madmen, intellectuals, and academic scribblers: The economic engine of political change*. Stanford University Press.

Majone, G. (1992). *Evidence, argument, and persuasion in the policy process*. Yale University Press.

Mahon, R. (2007). Swedish model dying of Baumols? Current debates. *New Political Economy, 12*, 79–85.

Marchlewska, M., Cichocka, A., Panayiotou, O., Castellanos, K., & Batayneh, J. (2018). Populism as identity politics: Perceived in-group disadvantage, collective narcissism, and support for populism. *Social Psychological and Personality Science, 9*(2), 151–162.

Margalit, Y. (2019). Economic insecurity and the causes of populism, reconsidered. *Journal of Economic Perspectives, 33*(4), 152–170.

Marx, K. (1867). *Das Kapital*, Erster Band, MEW, Bd, 23, 647. Vol 2. Hegel and Marx. Routledge.

McCloskey, D. (1985). *The rhetoric of economics*. University of Wisconsin Press.

McCloskey, D. (2006). *The bourgeois virtues: Ethics for an age of commerce*. University of Chicago Press.

Milanovic, B. (2016). *Global inequality: A new approach for the age of globalization*. Harvard University Press.

Mintrom, M. (1997). Policy entrepreneurs and the diffusion of innovation. *American Journal of Political Science, 41*(3), 738–770.

Moffitt, B. (2016). *The Global Rise of Populism: Performance, Political Style, and Repression*. Stanford University Press.

Mounk, Y. (2018). *The people vs. democracy: Why our freedom is in danger and how to save it*. Harvard University Press.

Mudde, C. (Ed.). (2017). *The populist radical right: A reader*. Routledge.

Mudde, C., & Kaltwasser, C. R. (Eds.). (2012). *Populism in Europe and the Americas: Threat or corrective for democracy?* Cambridge University Press.

North, D. C. (1981). *Structure and change in economic history*. Norton Press.

North, D. C. (1990). *Institutions, institutional change, and economic performance*. Cambridge University Press.

North, D. C. (1994). Economic performance through time. *The American Economic Review, 84*(3), 359–368.

Norris, P., & Inglehart, R. (2019). *Cultural backlash: Trump, Brexit, and authoritarian populism*. Cambridge University Press.

Noury, A., & Roland, G. (2020). Identity politics and populism in Europe. *Annual Review of Political Science, 23*(1), 421–439.

O'Connor, N. (2017). Three connections between rising economic inequality and the rise of populism. *Irish Studies in International Affairs, 28*, 29–43.

Olson, M. (1965). *The logic of collective action; public goods and the theory of groups*. Harvard University Press.

Olson, M. (1982). *The rise and decline of nations: Economic growth, stagflation, and social rigidities*. Yale University Press.

Piketty, T. (2014). *Capital in the 21st century*. Harvard University Press.

Putnam, R. (2020). *The upswing: How America came together a century ago and how we can do it again*. Simon & Schuster.

Roberts, K. M. (1995). Neoliberalism and the transformation of populism in Latin America: The Peruvian case. *World Politics, 48*(1), 82–116.

Rodrik, D. (2018). Populism and the economics of globalization. *Journal of International Business Policy, 1*(1), 12–33.

Rodrik, D. (2021). Why does globalization fuel populism? Economics, culture, and the rise of right-wing. *Populism Annual Review of Economics, 13*(1), 133–170.

Roosma, F., Gelissen, J., & van Oorschot, W. (2013). The multidimensionality of welfare state attitudes: A European cross-national study. *Social Indicators Research, 113*(1), 235–255.

Rosenberg, N., & Birdzell, L. E., Jr. (1987). *How the West grew rich: The economic transformation of the industrial world*. Basic Books.

Sabatier, P. A., & Zafonte, M. (2001). Policy knowledge: Advocacy organizations. In N. J. Smelser & B. Baltes (Eds.), *International Encyclopedia of the social and behavioral sciences* (pp. 11563–11568). Elsevier.

Sabatier, P., & Weible, C. (2007). The advocacy coalition framework: Innovations and clarifications. In P. Sabatier (Eds.), *Theories of the policy process* (2nd ed., pp. 189–222). Westview Press.

Scharpf, A. (2020). Dangerous alliances: Populists and the military. *GIGA Focus Latin America*, No. 1.

Schumpeter, J. A. (1942 [1994]). *Capitalism, socialism and democracy*. Routledge.

Shayegh, J., Storey, L., Turner, R., & Barry, J. (2021). A social identity approach to how elite outgroups are invoked by politicians and the media in nativist populism. *Social Psychology, 43*(6), 1009–1025.

Sniderman, P., & Hagendoorn, L. (2007). *When ways of life collide: Multiculturalism and its discontents in the Netherlands*. Princeton University Press.

Steinmayr, A. (2021). Contact versus exposure: Refugee presence and voting for the far-right. *The Review of Economics and Statistics, 103*(2), 310–327.

Sumpter, D. (2018). *Outnumbered: From Facebook and Google to fake news and filter-bubbles–the algorithms that control our lives*. Bloomsbury Sigma, Bloomsbury Publishing.

Tumber, H., & Waisbord, S. (2021). *The Routledge companion to media disinformation and populism*. Routledge.

Velasco, A. (2020). Populism and identity politics. *LSE Public Policy Review, 1*(1), 1–8.

Weyland, K. (1996). Neopopulism and Neoliberalism in Latin America: Unexpected Affinities. *Studies in Comparative International Development, 31*(3), 3–31.

Weyland, K. (2017). Populism: A political-strategic approach. In K. Weyland, C. R. Kaltwasser, P. Taggart, P. Espejo, & P. Ostiguy (Eds.), *The Oxford handbook of populism* (pp. 48–72). Oxford University Press.

Weyland, K. (2022). How populism dies: Political weaknesses of personalistic plebiscitarian leadership. *Political Science Quarterly, 137*(1), 9–42.

Williamson, O. E. (2000). The new institutional economics: Taking stock, looking ahead. *Journal of Economic Literature, 38*(3), 595–613.

CHAPTER 5

The Populist Divisive, Activist Ideas

Abstract In this chapter the ideational roots of the populist ideas are traced back to thinkers like Rousseau, Nietzsche, Heidegger, and Carl Schmitt, later to be developed within post-modernism and critical theory. Identity politics, as a politics of resentment and recognition, and as a function of meaning, community, and virtue are discussed and analyzed. I argue that populism, on both the left and the right, is a kind of collectivistic identity politics that appeals to the 'people' by constructing narratives that give a sense of belonging and by offering a purpose and meaning.

Keyword Populism · Populist ideas · Identity politics · Collectivistic identity politics · Post-modernism · Critical theory

Populism can be thus characterized as a specific set of political strategies which use a distinct rhetorical style or discursive frame to gain power and change the institutional orientation of society in a non-liberal, autocratic direction. To frame political issues in such a way that they affect the identity of people is at the core of the political strategies that populists use.

This involves the use of narratives that discursively "construct" the people and their different enemies. The narratives typically involve a

N. Karlson, *Reviving Classical Liberalism Against Populism*,
Palgrave Studies in Classical Liberalism,
https://doi.org/10.1007/978-3-031-49074-3_5

demand for respect and recognition of the lives of ordinary, hard-working people, who are said to be left behind and ignored by different elites and experts. These strategies are based on several divisive, activist ideas and the deliberate denial of rational discourse, objectivity, and truth. These ideas originate, as we shall see, from thinkers like Jean-Jacques Rousseau, Friedrich Nietzsche, Martin Heidegger, and Carl Schmitt, later to be developed within post-modernism and critical theory, to form the basis for both left- and right-wing populism. It is a kind of collectivistic identity politics that is hard to reconcile with classical liberalism.

A POLITICS OF RESENTMENT AND RECOGNITION

Identity politics is a loose concept. It emerged in the US to describe the civil rights movements in the 1960s with leaders like Martin Luther King. According to Kenny (2004), identity politics later typically became used to highlight new kinds of social mobilization based upon various group or collective identities that were previously hidden, suppressed, or neglected. Women's and gay liberation movements are the two most prominent examples. Just lately has it been connected to populism (Müller, 2016).

However, over time identity politics has more often been associated with political activism by various groups demanding special recognition for their unique experience. From having been a politics of equality of dignity, it developed into a politics of difference, to use the words of Talyor (1994)—everyone should be recognized for his or her unique identity. He argued that much of political discourse was driven by the invocation of recognition, from nationalist movements to demands on behalf of minority or subaltern groups in feminism and multiculturalism. Our identity is partly shaped, he argued, by recognition or its absence, and failures of recognition can cause real harm: misrecognition is not just a lack of due respect, but a vital human need.

According to his analysis, "the politics of recognition" is a major force in modern societies, demanding both the equal dignity and treatment of all citizens and a "politics of difference" which emphasizes that everyone is owed recognition of the unique identity of each individual or group. Populism can be said to be driven by both, when large groups feel resentment because, on the one hand, they are not equally recognized or respected, or, on the other, if they do not get sufficient recognition for the unique identity of their group. Critical theory has had a key role in the shift towards a politics of difference, supporting various LGBTQ movements, BlackLivesMatter, and other groups that were considered (relatively) deprived. Identity politics has also been used to describe separatist movements in Canada and Spain, or even as a synonym to multiculturalism (Bernstein, 2005; Izenberg, 2016).

Similarly, Fukuyama (2018) argues that humans do not just want things that are external to themselves, but also crave positive judgments about their worth or dignity, recognized by others. This—which he terms "thymos" building on the classical Greek concept—he believes is the reason behind today's identity politics, ranging from movements like MeToo and BlackLivesMatter to nationalism and populism. The quest for equal recognition from groups that have been marginalized in their societies, he argues, has been taken over by populist leaders like Donald Trump by frontally taking on "political correctness" to appeal to working-class supporters that feel they have been disregarded by national elites.

Another version of the same type of argument is Sandel's (2020) suggestion that today's societies' left-liberal consensus on meritocracy, and especially on the importance of higher education, has generated resentment among those left behind. Similarly, Goodhart (2017) argues that society is divided into two camps: 'anywheres', with careers and education, who travel the word, and 'somewheres', who get their identity from their local community and who feel forgotten and unrecognized due to social changes and globalization.

The Ideas Behind the Populist Strategies

The ideas behind the populist strategies have their origin in Jean-Jacques Rousseau who in *Du Contrat Social; ou Principes du Droit Politique* (1762) gave legitimacy to the populist project of autocratization by claiming that politics should be an expression of the *volonté general* (general will) of the people (Riker, 1982). The collective will of the people would be subverted and should not be restrained by checks-and-balances, judicial review, division of powers, minority rights, and the like, and thus the state had no limits.

However, the distinct rhetorical style or discursive frame originated with some German philosophers and political thinkers. Friedrich Nietzsche and Martin Heidegger cleared the ground by arguing that truth was a construct that could be changed by will. Rationality and reason should be replaced by emotions and the will to power. Carl Schmitt explained how political polarization and existential threats could be used to mobilize supporters.

Later post-modernists and critical theorists added additional elements to the populist rhetoric and strategies. In contrast to the modernism that originated with enlightenment philosophers and scientists like Descartes, Bacon, Locke, and Smith, post-modernists do not believe in reason, experience, and empirical evidence as sources of truth. Instead, post-modernists hold a social-linguistic, constructivist account of reality (Butler, 2002; Hicks, 2004). The "truth" and reality are viewed as constructed and contingent on historical, linguistic, and social contexts. This provided the basis for identity politics, but also cleared the ground for accusations of fake news. According to Foucault (Elden, 2021) and Derrida (Behler, 1991), leading contributors to post-modernism, Nietzsche and perhaps, in particular, his *The Genealogy of Morals* (1887 [1998]), has inspired what has been called "perspectivism", the idea that knowledge and truth always are bound to the interpretive perspectives of the observers, i.e., there are no universal truths. Reality can be "constructed" and "deconstructed" (Koelb, 1990).

Martin Heidegger, the existentialist philosopher, and Nazi, in turn, was the predecessor to the radical Frankfurter school (Lafont, 2018). He extended the ideas of Nietzsche in several dimensions, perhaps of particular relevance here by adding an antagonistic dimension. He argued that:

> An enemy is each and every person who poses an essential threat to the Dasein of the people and its individual members. ... (The challenge) is to bring the enemy to the open, to harbor no illusion about the enemy, to keep oneself ready for attack ...with the goal of total annihilation. (Heidegger 2010 [1934]: 73)

However, it was Carl Schmitt, the prominent legal scholar, and member of the Nazi party, deeply influenced by both Nietzsche and Heidegger, who formulated the populist strategy of polarization. In *The Concept of the Political* (Schmitt, 1932 [1996]: 26–27) he argued that the essence of politics is the creation of a conflict between friends and enemies:

> The specific political distinction to which political actions and motives can be reduced is that between friend and enemy. ... the political enemy need

not be morally evil or aesthetically ugly... But he is, nevertheless, the other, the stranger....

The conflict is existential, the enemy is whoever is "in a specially intense way, existentially something different and alien".

As both Schmitt and Rousseau agree, the people cannot be represented, because they would thereby renounce their sovereignty. In Schmitt's view, markets, civil society, and the rights of individuals are subordinated to the state, and even dictatorship would be legitimate in times of crisis. And a crisis was an opportunity not to be wasted.

To these activist ideas, Horkheimer, Marcuse, and other members of the Frankfurter school later added Gramscian Marxism and Freudian psychology to make their project explicitly radical left-leaning (Wiggershaus, 1994). The same is true for today's two most prominent theorists of populism, Ernesto Laclau and Chantal Mouffe, who both work in the traditions of post-modernism and critical theory.

Critical theory, originating in the Frankfurter school, shares many of the ideas presented above but also seeks "to liberate human beings from the circumstances that enslave them", as Horkheimer (1982: 244) put it. It is a social theory with the ambition of criticizing and changing society and existing power structures, not only to understand or explain things in the way normal social science tries to. To both post-modernism and critical theory there are grand (or meta) narratives that legitimize existing power structures that should be replaced by narratives that can activate the "lived experiences" of underprivileged social groups. These are the traditions that make up the ideational background of today's "woke" culture at numerous university campuses around the world, where scholars and students who defend alternative views are accused of "hate speech" and are "canceled".

Beiner (2018) has shown that the ideas of Nietzsche and Heidegger also play a crucial role for the populists on the far right. He traces the roots of such right-wing ideologues as Richard Spencer, Aleksandr Dugin, and Steve Bannon to the writings of these two philosophers, in particular to the aspects of their revulsion for modernity and the liberal-democratic view of life. This is a tradition that goes back to the so-called "conservative revolution" of the first decades of the twentieth century (Palmer, 2022; Woods, 1996).

In several influential contributions, Laclau and Mouffe have developed these ideas into an elaborate theory of populism, explaining how the 'people' and their adversaries can be deliberately "constructed" by activist movements; how to use the 'us-versus-them' logic to create a polarized antagonism and a direct relationship with people; and how democracy should be radicalized and the "neoliberal" narrative abolished to support a new "hegemonic" view of equality (see Laclau & Mouffe, 1985; Laclau, 2005; Mouffe 2018).

It should be noted that Mouffe explicitly bases her ideas on Carl Schmitt (Mouffe, 2005), which is also true for some of the right-wing populists (Abts & Rummens, 2007; Bergem & Bergem, 2019), possibly through the ideas of Leo Strauss (Meier, 1995). Laclau is also clearly influenced by Schmitt (Camargo, 2013). Most likely, the ideational connections between these varieties of populism are stronger than may be expected.

The connections between post-modernism, critical theory, and populism are multifaceted. First, post-modernism and critical theory is closely linked to identity politics and multiculturalism, as pointed out by Fukuyama (2018, 2022). When different groups and minorities, be they real or constructed, want their identities, and lived experiences to be recognized and respected, it is not only a question of equal rights but also about special rights based on race, sex, gender, or some other characteristic, fostering a culture of perpetual offense and victimhood. Second, the view that "truth" and reality are constructed opened up opportunities for populists' critique and allegations of media's "fake news". Third, if our interpretation of reality is made up of competing narratives, it takes just a small step to criticize the establishment's "political correctness" and support different conspiracy theories and allegations of fraud elections. Fourth, we have the case of Laclau and Mouffe who not only developed but also actively supported populist political strategies.

A basic problem. however, in the discussion about identity politics is that "identity" itself seldom is defined. So, what is identity, and how can it be defined?

IDENTITY AS A FUNCTION OF MEANING, COMMUNITY, AND VIRTUE

A need for identity is a fundamental human characteristic. Without identity, humans are deprived of a sense of belonging, and may also lack a purpose in life, character, pride, and self-esteem, all with negative consequences for mental well-being, physical health, etc. (Zika & Chamberlain, 1992). Identity is distinct from interests in the instrumental, material, or economic sense that economists usually use the term. Even though one could interpret identity as just a preference among others, such an analysis does not add to our understanding of the importance identity has for human behavior. In my understanding, humans are just as much identity-seeking creatures as they are rational in the economic sense.

Identity has many dimensions: individual, social, and collective. Personal or individual identity, in psychology, concerns our understanding of who we are, a sense of personal continuity and of uniqueness from other people. It is both backward and forward-looking, integrating the experiences, character, and ambitions of the individual. Individual identity is thus the self-understanding of a person. People also acquire social identities based on their membership in various communities or groups—familial, ethnic, occupational, and others, that help them define themselves in the eyes of both others and themselves (Erikson, 1950). According to Tajfel and Turner (1979) a person can have one personal but several social identities. For example, a person may hold various identities such as a teacher, father, or friend, based on different networks of organized relationships and communities. In this sense, we may thus have multiple identities. If one such social identity becomes more salient than the personal identity, people see themselves less as unique individuals and more as the proto-typical representative of their in-group (Van Stekelenburg, 2013).

Apart from individual and social identities psychologists speak of collective identities at the collective group level, which concerns the shared definition of a group that derives from members' common interests, experiences, and solidarity (Taylor & Whittier, 1992). Cultural identity is a type of collective identity. According to Klandermans and de Weerd (2000), group identification forms the link between collective and social identity, and thus the bridge between the individual and collective level of identity. To both left- and right-wing populists, collective identities have a central role; they form the "we" in the 'us-versus-them' logic. At the extreme, the collective identity may dominate other identities of a person.

Collective identities are important for social and political movements (Bernstein, 1997). Such identities can be based on ideas about anything from ideology, religion, nationalism, gender, or some other worldview (Van Stekelenburg, 2013). To raise consciousness and mobilize group members, boundaries are drawn up between different "challenging" groups. As we have seen this is a theme picked up by the populists.

More generally, the quest for identity—individual, social, and collective—seems to be closely related to the basic human need for recognition and respect. If these are absent the identity of the individual or the group is threatened, with potentially negative consequences as pointed out by Taylor (1994) and Fukuyama (2018) referred to above. Consequently, as argued in the last chapter, identity, and culture may sometimes be an even more important explanatory variable than different interests.

The question is then how identities are formed. I shall argue that identity is a function of meaning, community, and virtue.

Meaning

According to several empirical studies, identity formation is closely linked to searching for and acquiring meaning in one's life (Negru-Subtirica et al., 2016). Traditionally, religion provided the foundation for the meaning for most people, which is still true for some but not for all, as already Nietzsche pointed out. But even though there is no generally accepted definition of what is meant by saying that something is meaningful or what is meant by having meaning in life, some common ground can be found both among philosophers and psychologists.

In philosophy, there are many diverse opinions about what is meaningful, from antiquity and onwards. However, according to a survey by Metz (2022), at least in recent decades there is a standard view that life's meaning is about intentional actions, which exhibit a high final value present in 'the good, the true, and the beautiful' and absent from the hypothetical lives of Sisyphus endlessly pushing his stone up the hill or of those in an Experience Machine. In other words, it is about purposeful action towards worthwhile ends.

For example, Wolf (2010) argues that having meaningfulness is an essential element in a fully satisfying life. To her "meaning in life consist in and arises from actively engaging in projects of worth ... when subjective attraction meets objective attractiveness, and one is able to do something about it" (Wolf, 2010: 26). In other words, meaning occurs when you do something that really engages you, something that you love doing, but something that also is "larger than yourself", i.e., something the value of which has its source outside yourself, something that you believe is "objectively" good. These are, according to Wolf, activities that lead to fulfillment or meaning. Smoking pot or doing a gigantic jigsaw puzzle are examples she gives that do not fit the criteria. Similarly, according to Bauhn (2020), meaning is something we get by identifying ourselves with valuable purposes.

Wolf adds that the value of engaging in projects that can be seen as having a certain kind of objective worth partly arises from an interest to see one's life as valuable in a way that can be recognized from an external point of view. This may contribute to one's self-esteem regardless of whether this is a conscious concern or not through social feedback.

In psychology, there are a couple of classical theorists who have addressed the issue of meaning, perhaps most prominently Viktor Frankl, Abraham Maslow, and Irvin Yalom. Frankl (2008) conceived meaning as a process of discovery and implies decision-making. It can be attained through creative, experiential, and attitudinal values that inspire individuals to produce, create and achieve, to love and appreciate beauty, and to face injustice with dignity. Although circumstances exert a powerful influence on the making and fulfilling of meaning, these are largely dependent on a person's attitude toward their circumstances. Maslow (1971) saw meaning as a "meta-motive", that becomes important only after the satisfaction of more basic needs. To him meaning is an intrinsic emergent motivational force in individuals dedicating themselves to some values, mission, or cause. Yalom (1980) saw meaning in life as a creative response, a commitment, to the world's meaninglessness. Humans essentially choose and create their own meaning. Individuals need to commit themselves wholeheartedly to their chosen meanings and purposes if they wish to avoid the anxiety of nihilism. Later empirical studies seem to confirm these theories. For example, having a sense of purpose, efficacy, clear values, and of positive self-worth have been found to contribute to meaningfulness (Baumeister & Wilson, 1996).

While what is meaningful differs for different people, it is clear that meaning is an important element in someone's identity. It involves doing and engaging in things that are valuable, that have a purpose, some mission or cause. Also, empirical results show an interesting connection between meaning and community: to be socially rejected and ostracized has been shown to reduce meaningfulness (Baumeister, 2022).

What populism does is to offer meaning, and a valuable purpose: to fight against dangerous enemies, elites, or 'others', real or constructed, that are believed to threaten the lives of ordinary people. It is a collectivistic meaning, in contrast to the individualistic and social purposes of a pluralist society.

Community

A second foundation for identity is community. Humans have a quest for community, for a sense of belonging, as argued by Nisbet (1953). Communities also form the context for what Bauhn (2017) has called a person's "normative identity", her beliefs not only about who she is, but what she ought to do because of who she is. We may here distinguish between smaller communities and larger collectives.

I shall define a community as a fairly small group of people who have informal, direct, long-lasting, and multi-dimensional relations with each other, which forms the basis for the emergence of social norms (Karlson, 1993 [2002, 2017]). Such norms for how to behave in relation to others are social in the sense that the benefits to oneself accrue only indirectly through the responses of others, and in the fact that they are shared with others. Typical examples of social norms are to be honest, to keep promises, to do one's share in common projects, to help others in need etc.

For social norms to be upheld the conditions of community, as defined above, are required—they resemble the conditions necessary for making reciprocal cooperation possible, sometimes called tit-for-tat, including giving sanctions of different kinds, where otherwise free-riding behavior would prevail. There is a large game theoretical literature supporting this conclusion, as well as empirical studies by Ostrom and others (Ostrom 1990). Typical examples of communities are families, workplaces, clubs, neighborhoods, and voluntary organizations of various sorts that together form what often is called civil society.

Communities should be distinguished from collectives, which are made up of large numbers of people who only have indirect relations with each other. Typical examples are here nations, classes, or even the 'people' itself. Being part of a collective may well give rise to sentiments of belonging since the members may share characteristics like a common language, history, religion, and the like. But a collective does not fulfill the conditions necessary for the emergence and sustenance of social norms. This distinction between communities and collectives partly resembles the German sociologist Ferdinand Tönnies' (1887) classical distinction between *gemeinschaft* and *gesellschaft*. He argues that in the former people have direct face-to-face relations with each other spontaneously giving rise to emotions and sentiment of belonging, while in the latter, typified by modern, cosmopolitan societies human relations are more impersonal and indirect.

A collective, however, while not having the characteristics of a community, with a shared history, language, and culture may nevertheless offer a sense of belonging and identity. Think for example of soccer supporters or members of political movements. Also, religion, nationalism, or culture more generally, as understood by the anthropologists referred to in the last chapter, may provide such meaning and belonging.

I have argued in Karlson (1993 [2002, 2017]) that the social norms of smaller communities may be maintained in larger settings, or collectives, if the norms are internalized into a person's identity (her normative identity), and if the different individuals belong to several overlapping communities, forming a network of communities, with cross-cutting cleavages. They may also be upheld by religion or some other shared belief system. However, if and when the underlying communities should disappear, the social norms in the collectives will eventually disappear as well. The same is likely to be true of the sense of belonging.

Populism offers this kind of collectivist sense of belonging to the nation, class, or some other larger group that is said to be threatened by external enemies or elites that are supposed to uphold an economic or social system that does not give the 'people' sufficient recognition or show it enough respect. This is perhaps particularly true of right-wing nativists or nationalists, but also of left-wing populists who construct classes and groups that are said to be unfairly treated.

Virtue

A third important part of identity concerns the character of a person, and the virtues that he or she holds. These are the individual's behavioral traits or qualities that are considered praiseworthy or morally good and contribute to a good life. Typical examples of such character traits are to be honest, just, benevolent, tempered, courageous, prudent, trustworthy, industrious, etc.

Virtues are learned by practicing them, and by reflecting on these practices, throughout life. Together with the social norms they contribute to a person's normative identity. Eventually, they turn into habits that become an integrated part of a person's character and identity (Snow, 2016). Annas (2011) has argued that virtues in this way are similar to learned practical skills. Once attained such character traits are stable, fixed, and reliable dispositions. If an agent possesses the character trait of honesty, we expect him or her to act honestly in all sorts of situations, even when it is difficult to do so. It is an integral part of the agent's identity.

There may be various kinds of virtues depending on the context in which the individual is situated. The virtues of a university professor, for example, are likely to be different from those of a mother, a poet, a businessman, or an athlete. This said, it is common to identify cardinal virtues, like the ones mentioned above. Sometimes Christian virtues such as faith, hope, and love are added (McCloskey, 2006). Virtues are since Aristotle regarded to lay between two vices, a vice of excess and a vice of defect. Courage, for instance, is contrasted with the vices of foolhardiness and cowardness. It is also possible to distinguish civic virtues that describe the character of a good participant in the system of government—the personal qualities associated with the effective functioning of the civil and political order.

According to Aristotle in the *Nichomachean Ethics* (350 BC) (Crisp, 2014) and many other virtue ethicists, the different virtues support each other and form the basis for a good life, or *human flourishing*, to be distinguished from hedonism, narcissism, or short-term preference satisfaction (LeBar, 2018). Since virtue is a life-long project of self-development, it may not require perfection or excellence, as many of the classical thinkers believed (Frede, 2015). Most virtue ethicists also recognize the importance of narratives to what it means to live a good life—a person does not just live; he or she lives a *life* (Ulatowski & van Zyl, 2021).

It should also be noted that there is a connection between virtue and community, as defined in the last section. Already Adam Smith in *The Theory of Moral Sentiments* (1757) argued that virtues and moral behavior arise through a process where we sympathize with others, putting ourselves so to speak in the other person's situation, which is only possible in situations similar to how I defined community above, in smaller groups with repeated interactions where we can identify with and recognize each other. Through such a process, humans, according to Smith, develop an "internal observer" that also judges the morality or virtuousness of our behavior.

In recent decades, there has been a cross-fertilization between virtue ethics and developmental and cognitive psychology (Lapsley, 1996; Swanton, 2016), which has added substantial empirical support to the claim that character formation has substantial importance not only for morality and a good life in terms of satisfaction and fulfillment but also in terms of mental and physical health. Sometimes this is labeled a "positive psychology" of what makes life most worth living (Peterson & Seligman, 2004; Seligman, 1991).

Now, a central thesis of communitarian philosophers such as Charles Taylor (1989), Michael Sandel (1982), and Alisdair MacIntyre (1984) is that the development of virtue requires community. However, in the terminology adopted here what they often ask for is really a larger collective with a shared understanding both of the good for man and the good of the collective (Gutmann, 1985). They argue that modernity meant the end of a common teleological idea that human life had a proper end or understanding of the good, be it religious, republican or something else. And therefore, they claim, society has lost its moral foundation. Instead of a liberal "politics of rights", they favor "politics of the common good" (Sandel, 1996), based on settled traditions and established identities.

It is on this latter interpretation, the belief that a common end or common good is required for society to develop in the "correct" moral direction that populism relates to virtues. It is a virtue ethics from above, in contrast to the more individualistic and developmental-behavioral traits or qualities that were presented in the preceding paragraphs.

A COLLECTIVISTIC IDENTITY POLITICS

The populists' appeal to the true 'people' is a way to create engagement and support, in a comparable way to any social movement's appeal to a group's identity. In this sense populism is always a form of identity politics: it uses identity as a mean to get into power. An important feature is that some people are excluded (Müller, 2016), in a similar way to the movements supported by critical theorists mentioned above. It is not equal recognition or rights that are demanded, but privileges based on the uniqueness and special experience of the group that shares the identity in question. For populism, however, it is the 'people', or at least a majority of it, that request special treatments. The Hindu populism of Modi, who governs over more than a billion people in India, is a perhaps an extreme example, but the same is true for nationalist populists in Poland, Hungary, and many other countries.

Interestingly, the social democratic ideology of the welfare state that for most of the second half of the twentieth century dominated the political development of the Western world is another example of this kind of constructs (Karlson, 2019). This was especially so in Scandinavia where social democratic parties dominated policymaking and the political arena. But also, in Austria, Germany, and many other parts of continental Europe the same kind of ideas had a stronghold, albeit sometimes with a Christian democratic or social conservative framing. These welfare states not only promised social protection and government support of social services from cradle to grave, the ideology of the welfare state also provided a comprehensive vision of an ideal that was said to be morally superior to markets and a liberal society. For example, T. H. Marshall in his influential 1950 lectures *Citizenship and Social Class* argued that the welfare state is a prerequisite for social rights and social citizenship (Marshall, 1950). The Swedish economist Assar Lindbeck even claimed that the welfare state was a "major achievement of modern civilization" (Lindbeck, 1993: 97).

The narrative of the welfare state ideals in this way provided meaning and a sense of collective belonging and pride to the majority of the electorates in many Western democracies. Klein (2005) has called these welfare state ideas "the people's romance" and argues that this kind of political arrangements offer the romantic notion that "we're all working together", creating an encompassing sense of community, making people support the expansion of the state beyond rational argumentation. Buchanan (2005) in a somewhat similar way explained the support of the welfare state as an urge for "parentalism", meaning "the attitudes of persons who seek to have values imposed upon them by other persons, by the state or by transcendental forces" (Buchanan, 2005: 23).

The populists offer something similar. Their constructed conception of identity and identity politics is, as indicated above, primarily collectivistic or group oriented. It appeals to the 'people' by constructing narratives that give a sense of belonging, to the nation, class, religion, or some other trait, and by offering a worthy purpose and meaning, namely, to defend the people against enemies like corrupt elites or threatening others. They argue that to do so is a kind of virtue in the name of the common good. Note however that this is *not* a personal virtue like the cardinal virtues discussed earlier, it is rather a value or belief that is promoted from above.

In terms of meaning, populists offer a cause that is larger than the individual herself. This gives a collective sense of belonging, a sense of pride, that may boost self-esteem and a sense of dignity. Just to give one example, think of the Yellow Vests in France, uniting a remarkably diverse set of protesters. The collective identity may even dominate any personal identity and even group identity. This is the essence of the populists' politics of recognition. People are "seen" when they rally at mass meetings, participate in campaigns, or when their leader talks directly to them via television, Twitter, or other social media.

It is noteworthy that the populist identity politics as interpreted here is not—at least not in the longer run—compatible with community in the sense of small groups of people who have informal, direct, long-lasting, and multi-dimensional relations with each other, which forms the basis for the emergence of social norms. Neither is it compatible with individual virtue and character, as the examples of many populists' leaders' behavior and "flaunting of the 'low'" indicate. The populist, collective identity dominates and undermines individual character and long-term relationships in communities, as I have argued above.

An important element of this kind of collectivist identity is to have strong opinions about certain values and about what a good life is, and the conviction that it is legitimate to use the state to promote them. Since they, the true people, and their leader, represent the *volonté general* and the will of the majority no restrictions should apply. In the case of left-wing populists, this typically involves substantial redistribution to promote equality of outcomes, while for right-wing populists it instead often involves regulations to promote traditional social values towards Christianity, homosexuality, and immigrants. The good becomes politicized.

In both versions, the populist offer, as part of their narratives, polarized recognition but most often also unserious and ill-founded policies as well as various kinds of encroachments of the rule of law and constitutional democracy to favor their favorite ideas, be it protectionism, restrictions on pluralism or markets, or support of redistribution and expansive welfare program.

As briefly pointed out earlier, this is not something entirely new. This kind of populist identity politics is typical of Marxists' and socialists' deliberate framing of class struggles—one class being virtuous, the other greedy and corrupt. It was also the rhetoric used by the radical conservatives and fascists in the 1920s and 1930s when they hailed the heroic history of their nations and attacked and exterminated minorities and other "enemies to the people". Deliberately constructed narratives, symbols, and propaganda were prevalent. The same is to a considerable extent true for conservatives and nationalists who frame history, ethnicity, traditions, and national culture as being threatened by foreign forces or immigrants. For a comparison between fascism and right-wing populism, see Rydgren (2018). A leader like Vladimir Putin in Russia is using exactly this kind of rhetorical framing and arguments, just a Hugo Chavez and Nicolás Maduro in Venezuela. In fully autocratic polities such as China, North Korea, and most of the Arabic world it is just as visible. Islamism is populist identity politics taken to the extreme.

What is noteworthy is how prevalent tendencies of this type of politics have become also within Western democracies. As argued in the last chapter, digital social media undermining the belief in truth and the ability to activate the "tribal mind" are likely to have had important roles in this process. It is apparent that populist, collectivistic identity politics is attractive to many, and therefore a serious threat to liberty and the open society. The question is what can be done about it?

REFERENCES

Abts, K., & Rummens, S. (2007). Populism versus democracy. *Political Studies, 55*(2), 405–424.

Annas, J. (2011). *Intelligent virtue*. Oxford University Press.

Bauhn, P. (2017). *Normative identity*. Rowman & Littlefield International.

Bauhn, P. (2020). *Leva fritt & leva väl. En studie i moral, mening och mänskliga rättigheter*. Fri Tanke.

Baumeister, R. F. (2022). Psychological approaches to life's meaning. In I. Landau (Ed.), *The Oxford handbook of meaning in life* (pp. 416–430). Oxford University Press.

Baumeister, R. F., & Wilson, B. (1996). Life stories and the four needs for meaning. *Psychological Inquiry, 7*(4), 322–325.

Behler, E. (1991). *Confrontations: Derrida/Heidegger/Nietzsche*. Stanford University Press.

Beiner, R. (2018). *Dangerous minds: Nietzsche, Heidegger, and the return of the far right*. University of Pennsylvania Press.

Bergem, I. M., & Bergem, R. M. (2019). The political theology of populism and the case of the Front National. *Philosophy and Social Criticism, 45*(2), 186–211.

Bernstein, M. (1997). Celebration and suppression: The strategic uses of identity by the lesbian and gay movement. *American Journal of Sociology, 103*(3), 531–565.

Bernstein, M. (2005). Identity politics. *Annual Review of Sociology, 31*(1), 47–74.

Buchanan, J. (2005). Afraid to be free: Dependency as desideratum. *Public Choice, 124*(1–2), 19–31.

Butler, C. (2002). *Postmodernism*. Oxford University Press.

Camargo, R. (2013). Rethinking the political: A genealogy of the "antagonism" in Carl Schmitt through the Lens of Laclau-Mouffe-Žižek. *The New Centennial Review, 13*(1), 161–188.

Crisp, R. (Ed.). (2014). *Aristotle: Nicomachean ethics*. Cambridge University Press.

Elden, S. (2021). *The early Foucault*. Polity Press.

Erikson, E. H. (1950). *Childhood and society*. Norton.

Frankl, V. (2008). *Man's search for meaning*. Ebury Publishing.

Frede, D. (2015). Aristotle's virtue ethics. In L. Besser-Jones & M. Slote (Eds.), *The Routledge companion to virtue ethics* (pp. 17–30). Routledge, Taylor & Francis Group.

Fukuyama, F. (2018). *Identity: Contemporary identity politics and the struggle for recognition*. Profile books.

Fukuyama, F. (2022). *Liberalism and its discontents*. Profile Books.

Goodhart, D. (2017). *The road to somewhere: The populist revolt and the future of politics*. Oxford University Press.

Gutmann, A. (1985). Review: Communitarian critics of liberalism. *Philosophy & Public Affairs, 14*(3), 308–322.

Heidegger, M. (2010 [1934]). *Being and truth*. Indiana University Press.

Hicks, S. R. C. (2004). *Explaining postmodernism: Skepticism and socialism from Rousseau to Foucault*. Scholarly Publishing, Inc.

Horkheimer, M. (1982). *Critical theory selected essays*. Continuum Publishing.

Izenberg, G. N. (2016). *Identity: The necessity of a modern idea*. University of Pennsylvania Press.

Karlson, N. (1993 [2002, 2017]). *The state of state. An inquiry concerning the role of invisible hands in politics and civil society*. Almquist & Wiksell International. (Also published by Transaction Press, New Brunswick & London, with a new preface, 2002, and by Routledge, London 2017).

Karlson, N. (2019). The idea Vacuum of liberalism and the quest for meaning and community. *Journal of Contextual Economics—Schmollers Jahrbuch, 139*(2–4), 259–269.

Kenny, M. (2004). *The politics of identity: Liberal political theory and the dilemmas of difference*. Polity Press.

Klandermans, B., & De Weerd, M. (2000). Group identification and political protest. *Self, Identity, and Social Movements, 13*, 68–90.

Klein, D. (2005). The People's Romance: Why people love government (as much as thy do). *The Independent Review, 10*(1), 5–37.

Koelb, C. (1990). *Nietzsche as postmodernist: Essays pro and contra*. SUNY Press.

Laclau, E. (2005). *On populist reason*. Verso.

Laclau, E., & Mouffe, C. (1985). *Hegemony and socialist strategy. Towards a radical democratic politics*. Verso.

Lafont, C. (2018). Heidegger and the Frankfurt School. In P. E. Gordon, E. Hammer, & A. Honneth (Eds.), *The Routledge companion to the Frankfurt School* (pp. 282–294). Routledge.

Lapsley, D. K. (1996). *Moral psychology*. Westview.

LeBar, M. (Ed.). (2018). *Justice*. Oxford University Press.

Lindbeck, A. (1993). *The welfare state: The selected essays of Assar Lindbeck*. Edward Elgar.

MacIntyre, A. (1984). *After virtue: A study in moral theory* (2nd ed.). University of Notre Dame Press.

Marshall, T. H. (1950). *Citizenship and social class: And other essays*. University Press.

Maslow, A. H. (1971). *The farther reaches of human nature*. Viking Press.

McCloskey, D. (2006). *The Bourgeois virtues. Ethics for an age of commerce*. University of Chicago Press.

Meier, H. (1995). *Carl Schmitt and Leo Strauss: The hidden dialogue* (J. H. Lomax, Trans.). University of Chicago Press.

Metz, T. (2022). The concept of life's meaning. In I. Landau (Ed.), *The Oxford handbook of meaning in life* (pp. 27–42). Oxford University Press.

Mouffe, C. (2005). *On the Political*. Routledge.

Mouffe, C. (2018). *For a left populism*. Verso.

Müller, J. W. (2016). *What is populism?* University of Pennsylvania Press.

Negru-Subtirica, O., Pop, E. I., Luyckx, K., Dezutter, J., & Steger, M. F. (2016). The meaningful identity: A longitudinal look at the interplay between identity and meaning in life in adolescence. *Developmental Psychology, 52*(11), 1926.

Nietzsche, F. (1887 [1998]). *On the genealogy of morality*. Hackett Publishing.

Nisbet, R. (1953). *The quest for community: A study in the ethics of order and freedom*. Oxford University Press.

Ostrom, E. (1990). *Governing the commons: The evolution of institutions for collective action*. Cambridge University Press.

Palmer, T. (2022). Radical illiberalism on the right: The re-emergence of central themes of the 'conservative revolution'. Paper presented at the Mont Pelerin Society meeting in Oslo, October 2022.

Peterson, C., & Seligman, M. (2004). *Character strengths and virtues: A handbook and classification*. APA Press.

Riker, W. (1982). *Liberalism against Populism: A Confrontation between the Theory of Democracy and the Theory of Social Choice*. Freeman.

Rousseau, J. J. (1762). *Du contrat social; ou principes du droit politique*. Par JJ Rousseau, citoyen de Geneve. Edition sans cartons, à laquelle on a ajouté une Lettre de l'auteur au seul ami qui lui reste dans le monde. chez Marc-Michel Rey.

Rydgren, J. (Ed.). (2018). *The Oxford handbook of the radical right*. Oxford University Press.

Sandel, M. (1982). *Liberalism and the limits of justice*. Cambridge University Press.

Sandel, M. (1996). *Democracy's discontent. America in search of a public philosophy*. Belknap Press.

Sandel, M. (2020). *The tyranny of merit: What's become of the common good?* Farrar, Straus and Giroux.

Schmitt, C. (1932 [1996]). *The concept of the political*. Chicago: University of Chicago Press, 1996. Original publication (1st edition), Munich: Duncker & Humboldt.

Seligman, M. (1991). *Learned optimism: How to change your mind and your life*. Knopf.

Smith, A. (1757 [1982]). *The theory of moral sentiments*. Liberty Classics.

Snow, N. E. (2016). How habits makes us virtuous. In N. E. Snow, D. Narvaez, & J. Annas (Eds.), *Developing the virtues: Integrating perspectives* (pp. 135–156). Oxford University Press.

Swanton, C. (2016). Developmental virtue ethics. In N. E. Snow, D. Narvaez, & J. Annas (Eds.), *Developing the virtues: Integrating perspectives* (pp. 116–134). Oxford University Press.

Tajfel, H., & Turner, J. (1979). An integrative theory of intergroup conflict. In W. Austin & S. Worchel (Eds.), *The social psychology of intergroup relations* (pp. 33–47). Brooks/Cole Publishing Company.

Taylor, C. (1989). *Sources of the self: The making of the modern identity*. Harvard University Press.

Taylor, C. (1994). The politics of recognition. In A. Gutman (Ed.), *Multiculturalism* (pp. 25–73). Princeton University Press.

Taylor, V., & Whittier, N. E. (1992). Collective identity in social movement communities: Lesbian feminist mobilization. In A. D. Morris & C. M. Mueller (Eds.), *Frontiers in social movement theory* (pp. 104–129). Yale University Press.

Tönnies, F. (1887). *Gemeinschaft und Gesellschaft*. Berlin.

Ulatowski, J., & van Zyl, L. (Eds.). (2021). *Virtue, narrative, and self: Explorations of character in the philosophy of mind and action*. Routledge.

Van Stekelenburg, J. (2013). The political psychology of protest: Sacrificing for a cause. *European Psychologist, 18*(4), 224.

Wiggershaus, R. (1994). *The Frankfurt School: Its history, theories, and political significance*. Polity Press and MIT Press.

Wolf, S. (2010). *Meaning in life and why it matters*. Princeton University Press.

Woods, R. (1996). *The conservative revolution in the Weimar Republic*. St. Martin's.

Yalom, I. D. (1980). *Existential psychotherapy*. Basic Books.

Zika, S., & Chamberlain, K. (1992). On the relation between meaning in life and psychological well-being. *British Journal of Psychology, 83*(1), 133–145.

CHAPTER 6

The Classical Liberal Ideas, Predicaments, and Potentials

Abstract In this chapter classical liberalism, and different liberal predicaments and potentials to fight back against populism, are explored. Liberals cannot resort to the same methods as the populists without abandoning liberalism itself. But the three dimensions of classical liberalism, about institutions, economics and society, and the liberal spirit reinforce each other and provide the potential for fighting back against populist threats.

Keyword Classical liberalism · Liberal predicaments · Liberal potentials · Liberal institutions · Liberal economy and society · the liberal spirit

How can liberals fight back against the populist threat to liberty, democracy, and the open society? What lessons can be drawn from the analysis in the previous chapters for how to stop democratic backsliding and voter support for populist parties? What kinds of strategies or measures can be developed to counter the rhetorical style, discursive frame, and institutional orientation of populism?

The world will not change for the better unless liberals start fighting back. As argued by John Gray, there is a liberal delusion: "the greatest danger for the west comes from the groundless faith that history is on its side" (Gray, 2014). The argument in this chapter is that liberals

© The Author(s) 2024
N. Karlson, *Reviving Classical Liberalism Against Populism*,
Palgrave Studies in Classical Liberalism,
https://doi.org/10.1007/978-3-031-49074-3_6

must develop or revitalize their own ideas, beliefs, and values to battle populism.

The rise of populism, as we saw in Chapter 4, can largely be explained by the popularity of populist ideas, the collectivistic identity politics explored further in Chapter 5. Another way to put this is to say that liberals have left an idea vacuum, by not sufficiently developing their own ideas, that the populist has filled (Karlson, 2019).

It is partly a question of insufficient policy responses to changes in economic and social conditions affecting voters. However, as was argued in Chapter 4, such changes need to be interpreted and understood as good or bad, as just or unjust, as beneficial or not, to have a causal effect. This means that more important, I will argue below, is to revive, revitalize and develop the ideas of liberalism itself. It is not only a question of communication. Modern liberals have largely neglected that humans have a quest for meaning, community, belonging, identity, and a purpose in life, that we are meaning-searching, meaning-creating animals.

In an essay, James Buchanan point to this weakness and argues that liberals have failed to "save the soul" of classical liberalism. He argues that the focus on economic efficiency and self-interest simply is not enough to secure public support. Instead: a vision of an ideal, over and beyond science and self-interest, is necessary he argues, and those who profess membership in the club of classical liberals have failed singularly in their neglect of this requirement (Buchanan, 2000: 112).

Still, there are no quick fixes or easy answers that would address information disorder, repair the civic fabric, or reestablish trust in politics and public discourse. Liberals may here face a predicament, in the sense that they have a more limited set of alternative means to use to gain and attain power than the populists.

The Liberal Predicaments

Adapting a phrase from Isaiah Berlin, Cherniss has formulated this "liberal predicament" as follows: "how to combat anti-liberal movements, which are not constrained in the way that liberal movements and regimes are, without either sacrificing political efficacy or betraying basic liberal principles in the name of defending them?" (Cherniss, 2021: 4–5).

Recall the populist strategies presented in Chapter 2. Liberals obviously do not want to move society in an autocratic direction, circumventing representative government, taking control of the courts, the public service, and media companies, and restricting media freedom, etc. Neither do they want to manipulate elections, abolish minority rights, constitutional constraints, and the rule of law to establish an illiberal democracy. Or for that matter, to promote their values and ideas of the good through government. Just as important, neither do liberals want to promote polarization, use the 'us-versus-them' logic, attack the establishment and different elites, or identify 'others' that threaten the existential identity of the 'true people', demonize opponents, attack media and science for producing lies and fake news. To flaunt the 'low', being intolerant and ruthless also go against what liberals believe and cherish. Neither do liberals want to resort to unserious and ill-founded policy solutions to complex social and economic problems to get elected. To put is short, liberals can hardly resort to the same methods as the populists without abandoning liberalism itself.

While this is certainly true, liberalism still possesses numerous strategies to fight back the populist threat. The potential strength of the classical liberal ideas about institutions, economics, and society, as well as what I shall call, the liberal spirit or ethos, should not be underestimated. It is time to revive, develop and defend some of these liberal ideas and traditions. Moreover, liberals need to invest more resources in policy entrepreneurs and political leaders that have the skills and ambitions to articulate and promote liberal policies in the political process.

In the coming chapters, several strategies for how to fight back against populism will be suggested. This requires no less than a revival of liberalism. First, however, the ideas of classical liberalism itself need to be examined.

THE THREE DIMENSIONS OF CLASSICAL LIBERALISM

Classical liberalism has a long, complex, and many-faceted history that goes back to the early days of the Enlightenment, to the Dutch republic in the Netherlands and the Glorious revolution in the United Kingdom, when science and rational argumentation started to replace superstition and prejudices, and when the first steps to secure freedom of thought, religion, and contract by limiting and focusing the powers of the state were taken. It is based on a broad idea tradition with numerous important contributors that go back at least to John Locke and his *Two Treaties on Government* published in 1689, who argued that all men are created equal, legitimate government rests on the consent of the people (Locke,

1689 [1988], and the protection of individual property rights provide the foundation for a civilized society. David Hume, Adam Smith, Immanuel Kant, Wilhelm von Humboldt, and John Stuart Mill, later followed by Friedrich Hayek, Karl Popper, Milton Friedman, Isiah Berlin, Robert Nozick, James Buchanan, Judith Shklar, William Galston, and many others developed and extended these ideas.

Classical liberalism is thus not a fixed doctrine. It is a tradition that has evolved over time and adapted to changing circumstances and challenges. In this sense, there have been many "neoliberalisms". For example, most of the famous participants at the meeting at Mont Pelerin in 1947, such as Friedrich Hayek, Milton Friedman, Wilhelm Röpke, Frank Knight, Karl Popper, George Stigler, Lionel Robbins, Michael Polanyi, and Walter Eucken saw themselves as reviving liberalism because they were critical of the "laissez-faire" liberalism of the preceding era that they believed had failed politically. Only Ludwig von Mises wished to retain the term. Some favored more extensive social policies and a "social market economy", while others had a more critical view of interventions into markets and civil society. While intensely disagreeing on several matters, they wanted policies and institutions that could solve problems of poverty, free markets, agriculture, education, peace, and international cooperation. This is far from the strawmen versions of "neoliberalism" created by left-wing populists and some more prominent social scientists referred to above. For a brilliant exposé of the discussions taking place at this founding meeting of the Mont Pelerin Society, see Caldwell (2022).

Classical liberals thus disagree on many important issues, not only about policies and the role of the state but also about the ethical or normative foundations of a liberal society. But they all agree that a liberal society is a free, open, and pluralistic society, contrary to an authoritarian society. Individual freedom and equal dignity are the fundamental values. As I understand it, classical liberalism has at least three dimensions or facets: one institutional, one economic and social, and one spiritual. The latter is often disregarded. Together they reinforce each other.

The Liberal Institutions

Most often liberalism is equated with certain principles and institutions, namely a strong preference for institutions that protect individual liberty and human dignity, through limited government, the rule of law, private property rights, civil liberties, and constitutional democracy. Liberalism in this sense is primarily a theory of the state, a political theory.

Liberals want the state to be neutral with respect to the *good*: the interpretation and exploration of what a good life entails are up to the individual, not the state. The state should secure the *rights* of individuals to develop their own lives through experience and reflection, in markets and in civil society, individually and together with others.

Classical liberals believe that the only good reason to restrict people's freedom is to prevent them from harming others. As argued by Shklar (1989), every adult should be able to make as many effective decisions without fear or favor about as many aspects of his or her life as is compatible with the like freedom of every adult. Individuals have rights that are universal but necessitate a strong but limited government. Governments should be constitutionally constrained through the division of powers, federalism, checks and balances, the principle of legality, judicial review, two-chamber parliaments, and similar mechanisms. A private sphere should be guaranteed.

Such a liberal or constitutional, democracy is different from a populist, or simply electoral, democracy. As argued by Riker (1982), a liberal democracy puts the emphasis on the legality principle (*lex superior*), the division of power, pluralism, minority veto, and federalism, in contrast, populist democracies on state sovereignty, parliamentarism, monism, majority rule, and a unitary state. The legality principle means that the government itself is under the law—the constitutional rules are superior to ordinary legislation. Pluralism is the opposite of monism. A monistic state is centralized and unitary, with no independent power centers. Both types of democracies have general elections based on a one-man-one vote.

Today's classical liberals are thus critical to the excessive growth of the state, redistribution, high taxes, and over-regulation, but also to the influence of special interests and crony capitalism. Almost all classical liberals in different ways favor public support for education and for those who are weak and vulnerable, as well as for a limited number of public goods such as infrastructure and environmental protection that would not be produced or secured at sufficient levels by markets and civil society organizations. Classical liberalism, however, needs to be distinguished from modern social liberalism, social democracy, and what Americans call "liberalism", which see no real limits to state action, taxation, and redistributive policies. I shall return to these questions below.

The Liberal Economy and Society

Just as often classical liberalism is equated with the economic and social consequences that follow from liberal principles and institutions, namely the characteristics of liberal societies such as voluntary cooperation, the market economy, civil society, and the open society. Private property rights with freedom of contract and freedom of establishment result in a competitive market process that leads to the wealth of nations, as Adam Smith (1776) put it. The market economy works as a discovery procedure that uses knowledge that would otherwise not have been discovered or used (Hayek, 1945, 1978). It is a society where the individual is free to choose (Friedman & Friedman, 1980). Therefore, a liberal society is characterized by prosperity, innovations, dynamism, and opportunity.

But liberal institutions, just as importantly, also provide the foundations for a civil society with clubs, voluntary organizations, families, and other forms of associations. This is a tradition that also goes back to the Scottish enlightenment with Adam Ferguson (1767), Adam Smith (1757), and others, later to be followed by Alexis de Tocqueville (1840), James Buchanan (1965), and others. As discussed in the last chapter, it is the communities in civil society that provide the conditions necessary for the emergence of social norms and social cohesion. In this way, in many situations, a free economy and civil society support each other. As shown by Berggren and Jordahl (2006) and Berggren and Nilsson (2016) economic freedom and the rule of law not only promote prosperity but also increases trust, social capital, and tolerance. And markets in many cases foster morality and virtues (Karlson et al., 2015; Storr & Choi, 2019). Notably, civil society also has the epistemic advantage that local knowledge is created and used (Lewis, 2013).

More generally, a liberal society with liberal institutions, free markets, and civil society is an open society. The term was coined by Henri Bergson (1932) to describe a modern, dynamic, pluralistic, and tolerant society, in contrast to a closed, clan society. It was Karl Popper (1945), however, who made the term popular. He contrasted tribalistic and collectivist societies—exemplified by fascism and socialism—to open, democratic societies that are based on rationality and public discussions, and personal responsibility and accountability for moral choices. According to Popper, an open society has no overall goal or predetermined end-state, it is characterized by uncertainty due to individual liberty, choice, and pluralism.

It should be emphasized that both markets and civil society are examples of spontaneous orders, to use the terminology of Hayek (1973). The overall order arises as an unintended consequence of human action, but not of human design. Both the coordination taking place in markets through the price mechanism and the social norms and virtues in civil society have arisen through the purposeful interactions of individuals and organizations within the system or rules provided by the liberal institutions and limited government described above, not through deliberate planning from above (Karlson, 1993 [2002, 2017]). This is also why liberal or constitutional, democracy is superior to any known alternatives in the longer run. Understanding how such spontaneous orders contribute to the creation of prosperity and the welfare of the citizens is far from intuitive to most people.

The Liberal Spirit

The third, less often emphasized, and more comprehensive dimension of classical liberalism is what I call "the liberal spirit", a term inspired by Montesquieu's *L'Esprit des Lois* (1748), "the spirit of the laws". Perhaps the expression "the liberal ethos" could be used just as well for what I am aiming at, but "spirit" is wider, not only covering questions of character and virtue. It should also be distinguished from "the liberal sentiment", a term used by Gustavsson (2023) denoting the romantic, emotional aspects of some liberal thinkers' ideas. Moreover, in my interpretation, the liberal spirit is not equivalent to the "free spirits" that, according to Pittz (2020), combat dogmatism and fanaticism and the putative authority of public opinion.

The liberal spirit is intended to denote the more general cultural identity of the kind of society that classical liberals favor. It is a society that rejoices in individual development and self-authorship, entrepreneurship and economic development, diversity and tolerance, mutual respect and recognition, free speech and rational discourse, science, and in voluntary cooperation, and in many different virtues, both personal and civic (see e.g., Galston, 1988; Macedo, 1990). It is an optimistic, future-oriented spirit. It is characterized by a moral of aspirations, to use Lon Fuller's term (1969).

The liberal spirit involves what McCloskey (2016, 2019) has called the *bourgeoisie virtues*. She emphasizes the importance of virtues that go beyond mere financial and personal prudence, encompassing social virtues and the Christian virtues of faith, hope, and love, for the explanation of the enormous increase in wealth and prosperity that has taken place over the last 200 and 300 years. The liberal spirit, however, is also intended to capture liberalism's ability to offer emancipation, meaning, and community, a sense of purpose, and belonging. In essence, the liberal spirit concerns human flourishing in a broad sense.

Hence, it is important to note that those classical liberals that embrace the liberal spirit are not, as Galston (1982) has pointed out, complete neutral to the good and the good life. But since what is valuable in life, the good, differs for different individuals, and since an open, pluralist society lacks an overall purpose and end, liberals need to be humble and tolerant. Liberals value many different versions of human flourishing, in contrast to those who favor perfectionism, in the sense that the good of man can be universally defined. Therefore, the liberal spirit is tempered and moderate, as argued by liberal thinkers like Raymond Aron, Reinhold Niebuhr, and Isaiah Berlin (Cherniss, 2021).

For example, liberalism is fully compatible with conservative lifestyles, such as the Amish in the US, as well as with decentralized "socialist" communities such as the Kibbutzim in Israel, as long as they do not limit the liberty of others. To be tolerant of what you may dislike is a key characteristic of the liberal spirit—the conditional acceptance of or non-interference with beliefs, actions, or practices that one considers to be wrong but still "tolerable," such that they should not be prohibited or constrained. As Mill argued in Chapter 2 of *On Liberty* (1859 [1975]) not even sexual immorality nor religious heresy warrants prohibition. This is also one reason liberals respect the rights of minorities against the will of the voter majority—also weaker groups should have the right to live on their own terms (see Craiutu, 2022).

As argued by Cherniss (2021), liberalism is the opposite of ruthlessness. He urges us to see liberalism not as a set of policies but as a temperament or disposition—one marked by an openness to complexity, willingness to acknowledge uncertainty, tolerance for difference, and resistance to ruthlessness. He believes this is especially important in dark times, such as ours, facing the threats of authoritarian populism.

THE LIBERAL POTENTIALS

FThese three dimensions, facets, or, perhaps, conceptions of classical liberalism reinforce each other. The optimistic but tempered liberal spirit supports both liberal institutions and the liberal economy and society. Markets and civil society, just as liberal democracy, and limited government, presuppose and are strengthened by citizens and actors on the markets that are virtuous, tempered, and cherish individual, social, and economic development. Liberal institutions, on their hand, support and provide mechanisms for diversity and tolerance, mutual respect, and rational discourse, just as they support markets, prosperity, and voluntary cooperation. And a liberal economy and society produce consequences that strengthen the liberal spirit and the liberal institutions. Together they provide the potential for fighting back at the populist threat.

Let me emphasize, however, that liberalism is never complete or perfect, it is not a utopia even if it may be said to have a distinct "soul". Liberal ideas, values, and beliefs can always be improved and developed to be better adapted to the changing circumstances and challenges of our societies. Our institutions, our economy and society, and our spirit are, and will never be, perfect or complete. They can always be developed and improved. Perhaps this is the most important reason behind the potential for liberalism to fight back against populism. It should not be underestimated.

I shall structure the counterstrategies to be suggested below under four broad headings:

- Expose the populist strategies and their consequences
- Defend and develop the liberal institutions
- Embracd and promote the liberal spirit
- Develop liberal statecraft

Under some of the headings, several sub-strategies will be proposed.

REFERENCES

Berggren, N., & Jordahl, H. (2006). Free to trust: Economic freedom and social capital. *Kyklos, 59*(2), 141–169.

Berggren, N., & Nilsson, T. (2016). Tolerance in the United States: Does economic freedom transform racial, religious, political and sexual attitudes? *European Journal of Political Economy, 45*, 53–70.

Bergson, H. (1932). *Les deux sources de la morale et de la religion.* Alcan.

Buchanan, J. (1965). An economic theory of clubs. *Economica. New Series, 32*(125), 1–14.

Buchanan, J. (2000). The soul of classical liberalism. *The Independent Review,* Summer 2000, V(1): 111–119.

Caldwell, B. (2022). *Mont Pèlerin 1947: Transcripts of the Founding Meeting of the Mont Pèlerin Society.* Hoover Institution Press.

Cherniss, J. (2021). *Liberalism in dark times: The liberal ethos in the twentieth century.* Princeton University Press.

Craiutu, A. (2022). *Why Are So Many Western Intellectuals Abandoning Liberalism and What Can We Do About It?* Paper presented at Mont Pèlerin Society, Oslo, Norway, October 8, 2022.

de Tocqueville, A. (1840). *Democracy in America.* Saunders and Otley.

Ferguson, A. (1767). *An essay on the history of civil society.* Printed by Boulter Grierson, printer to the King's most Excellent Majesty., MDCCLXVII.

Friedman, M., & Friedman, R. D. (1980). *Free to choose.* Harcourt Brace Jovanovich.

Fuller, L. (1969). *The morality of law.* Yale University Press.

Galston, W. (1982). Defending liberalism. *American Political Science Review, 76*(3), 621–629.

Galston, W. A. (1988). Liberal Virtues. *The American Political Science Review, 82*(4).

Gray, J. (2014, September 18). "Berlin Wall anniversary: 25 years of liberal delusion". *Prospect Magazine.* https://www.prospectmagazine.co.uk/essays/berlin-wall-anniversary-25-years-of-liberal-delusion

Gustavsson, G. (2023). *Det öppna sinnelaget – och dess fiender.* Stockholm: Fri tanke.

Hayek, F. A. (1945). The use of knowledge in society. *The American Economic Review., 35*(4), 519–530.

Hayek, F. A. (1973). *Law, Legislation and Liberty, Vol 1: Rules and Order.* Routledge & Kegan Paul.

Hayek, F. A. (1978). Competition as a discovery procedure. *New studies in philosophy, politics, economics and the history of ideas.* Routledge & Kegan Paul.

Karlson, N. (1993 [2002, 2017]). *The state of state. An inquiry concerning the role of invisible hands in politics and civil society.* Almquist & Wiksell International. (Also published by Transaction Press, New Brunswick & London, with a new preface, 2002, and by Routledge, London 2017).

Karlson, N. (2019). The idea vacuum of liberalism and the quest for meaning and community. *Journal of Contextual Economics—Schmollers Jahrbuch, 139*(2–4), 259–269.

Karlson, N., Wennberg, K., & Norek, M. (2015). *Virtues in entrepreneurship.* Ratio och Publit förlag.

Lewis, P. (2013). Hayek, social theory, and the contrastive explanation of socio-economic order. *Critical Review, 25*(3–4), 386–408.

Locke, J. (1988). *Two treatises of government*, Peter Laslett (ed.). Cambridge University Press.

Macedo, S. (1990). *Liberal virtues: Citizenship, virtue, and community in liberal constitutionalism.* Clarendon Press.

McCloskey, D. (2016). *Bourgeois equality: How ideas, not capital or institutions, enriched the worlds.* University of Chicago Press.

McCloskey, D. (2019). *Why liberalism wworks: How true liberal values produce a freer, more equal, prosperous world for all.* Yale University Press.

Mill, J. S. (1859 [1975]). *On Liberty*, Spitz, D. (eds.), Norton and Co.

Montesquieu, C. – L. de S. (1748). *De l'Esprit des Loix, ou du rapport que les loix doivent avoir avec la constitution de chaque gouvernement, mœurs, climat, religion, commerce, etc.* (sic); à quoi l'auteur a ajouté des recherches sur les lois romaines touchant les successions, sur les lois françaises et sur les lois féodales. Genève, Barrillot & Fils,

Pittz, S. (2020). *Recovering the liberal spirit: Nietzsche, individuality, and spiritual freedom.* State University of New York Press.

Popper, K. (1945). *The open society and its enemies.* Routledge.

Riker, W. (1982). *Liberalism against populism: A confrontation between the theory of democracy and the theory of social choice.* Freeman.

Shklar, J. (1989). The liberalism of fear. In N. L. Rosenblum (Ed.), *Liberalism and moral life* (pp. 21–38). Harvard University Press.

Smith, A. (1757[1982]). *The theory of moral sentiments.* Liberty Classics.

Smith, A. (1776). *An inquiry into the nature and causes of the wealth of nations: Volume One.* Printed for W. Strahan; and T. Cadell.

Storr, V. H., & Choi, G. S. (2019). *Do markets corrupt our morals?* Palgrave Macmillan.

CHAPTER 7

Expose the Populist Strategies and Their Consequences

Abstract In this short chapter the first counterstrategy to fight back against populists, both on the left and on the right, is presented. I argue that many supporters of populism are neither aware of the deliberate manipulation that lies behind the strategies used by populists, nor the negative consequences that follow for society at large, for democracy, and in the end for the supporters of the populists themselves. Hence, it is necessary to expose the populist strategies and to explain their consequences.

Keyword Counterstrategy against populism · Consequences of populism · Polarization · Manipulation

A first important counterstrategy to fight back against populists, both on the left and on the right, is to expose the deliberate strategies of polarization they use to gain power and change the institutional structure of society in an autocratic direction.

While apparently attractive to voters in many democracies—partly due to latent tribal minds and a media logic enhanced by social media—it is reasonable to think that many supporters of populism are neither aware of the deliberate manipulation that lies behind the strategies used by populists, nor the negative consequences that follow for society at

N. Karlson, *Reviving Classical Liberalism Against Populism*,
Palgrave Studies in Classical Liberalism,
https://doi.org/10.1007/978-3-031-49074-3_7

large, for democracy, and in the end for the supporters of the populists themselves.

The core idea, as explained in earlier chapters, is to construct a conflict between friends and enemies using the rhetorical style and discourse frame of the 'us-versus-them' logic. The 'we'—the people, who are considered to have a unified will, the volonté general—are just as the 'them'—the elites and the others—deliberately constructed to make the threat deeply existential. The 'we' is good, while the 'them' is evil and corrupt. Often a crisis or major economic and social changes are used to expose the failure of the enemies. The demonization of opponents, attacks on media and science, and intolerant and ruthless behavior serve the same purpose. Narratives and emotional arguments demand respect for and recognition of the 'people'. Rational arguments are dismissed, and conspiracies are supported. To the left, the populist narratives blame "neoliberalism", while on the right the narratives focus on immigration, multiculturalism, and political correctness, as the causes of all evil. Both sides use similar populist strategies to deliberately promote the polarization of politics and society. In many cases, they indirectly strengthen each other in a symbiotic way.

There is empirical evidence showing, at least in the US, that polarization among the elites is stronger than among the public. Mass polarization also came later (McCarty, 2019). In fact, there are indications that voters dislike polarization. In a PEW survey in 2021, one interesting result was that while the US turned out to be one of the most polarized countries, overwhelming majorities of both Trump (86%) and Biden (89%) supporters surveyed said that their preferred candidate, if elected, should focus on addressing the needs of all Americans, "even if it means disappointing some of his supporters." (Dimock & Wike, 2021). Voters also generally dislike politicians that lie and disregard facts (Janezic& Gallego, 2020). An indication of this, based on European data, is that political participation decreases in more polarized polities (Casal Bértoa & Rama, 2021).

In general, there is a great need to explain that the populist strategies are undermining democracies themselves in the longer run. The creeping autocratization that populists favor in the name of the majority of the 'true' people, with restrictions on the freedom of the press and the independence of the courts, means no less than the end of constitutional or liberal democracy and the open society.

Thus, exposing and explaining how populists deliberately promote the polarization of society, and the risk of autocratization that follows, could potentially be an important strategy for how to fight back against populism. Such a strategy should also be attractive to the more established political parties, rather than falling into the populist rhetorical trap themselves.

However, just as important is probably to expose the economic and social consequences of populist policies. The unserious and ill-founded policies the populists commonly advocate may seem to be attractive in the short run, but in the long run, the opposite is generally the case, as was explained in Chapter 2, also for those groups they are said to favor. In addition, as argued in Chapter 5, the collectivistic identity politics of populism is also likely to undermine social norms and individual virtues, and the sense of belonging that populism may appear to offer. This brings us over to the next counterstrategy.

REFERENCES

Casal Bértoa, F., & Rama, J. (2021). Polarization: What do we know and what can we do about it? *Frontiers in Political Science, 56*.

Dimock, M., & Wike, R. (2021, March 29). America is exceptional in its political divide: The pandemic has revealed how pervasive the divide in American politics is relative to other nations". *Trust Magazine*. America Is Exceptional in Its Political Divide | The Pew Charitable Trusts (pewtrusts.org). Gathered January 13, 2023.

Janezic, K., & Gallego, A. (2020). Eliciting preferences for truth-telling in a survey of politicians. *PNAS, 117*(36), 22002–22008.

McCarty, N. (2019). *Polarization: What everyone needs to know*. Oxford University Press.

Open Access This chapter is licensed under the terms of the Creative Commons Attribution 4.0 International License (http://creativecommons.org/licenses/by/4.0/), which permits use, sharing, adaptation, distribution and reproduction in any medium or format, as long as you give appropriate credit to the original author(s) and the source, provide a link to the Creative Commons license and indicate if changes were made.

The images or other third party material in this chapter are included in the chapter's Creative Commons license, unless indicated otherwise in a credit line to the material. If material is not included in the chapter's Creative Commons license and your intended use is not permitted by statutory regulation or exceeds the permitted use, you will need to obtain permission directly from the copyright holder.

CHAPTER 8

Defend and Develop the Liberal Institutions

Abstract In this chapter a second group of counterstrategies against populism is presented. I argue that it is necessary to defend, develop and improve the liberal institutions and policies in today's liberal democracies. These institutions need to be secured and given a better defense. The suggested counterstrategies include the improvement of liberal literacy; the securement of a strong, limited, and decent state; the support of federalism and decentralization; the stimulation of social mobility; the implementation of high-quality basic education; the strengthening of integration; and the restoration of public discourse.

Keywords Counterstrategy against populism · Liberal institutions · Liberal policies · Liberal literacy · Limited and decent state · Federalism · Integration · Public discourse

A second group of counterstrategies concerns the need to defend, develop and improve the liberal institutions and policies in today's liberal democracies. As explained in Chapter 4 changing economic and social conditions, especially if they turn into crises, often provide the background for why populist strategies may appear appealing to the voters. If the electorate is made to believe that their interests and identities are

N. Karlson, *Reviving Classical Liberalism Against Populism,*
Palgrave Studies in Classical Liberalism,
https://doi.org/10.1007/978-3-031-49074-3_8

threatened by real or perceived policy failures, it is not surprising that they lose faith in the established parties, elites, and experts.

It may well be that liberals had become complacent, even if not naively believing in the end of history (Fukuyama, 1989; 1992) and had forgotten Karl Popper's dictum about the necessity of continuous piecemeal reform to sustain open societies and liberal democracies (Popper, 1945). When economic and social conditions change, often institutions and policies need to change as well. In this sense, the populist critique may have been correct at least to a degree. To fight back liberalism needs a reform program.

It is easy to identify policy failures in all democracies. For example, there are legitimate complaints in many countries about the education system, law, and order, health care, welfare services, the cost of housing, infrastructure, energy prices, immigration policy, and many other areas— not to mention the challenges caused by climate change, the increasing share of elderly, etc. And perhaps worse of all when it comes to the support for populism: corruption.

Many of these problems should, could, and need to be fixed. While this is not the place to present a full reform program, a few suggestions concerning the promotion of social mobility, the strengthening of integration, and the restoration of public discourse will be outlined below. Importantly, the reforms needed to a considerable extent need to be adapted to the local conditions and challenges in the relevant societies and polities in question. However, it is crucial to distinguish between real and perceived or constructed failures, to understand why the problems have arisen in the first place, and by what methods or means they can be fixed.

Populists are, as argued above, often willing to promote simplistic answers to complex questions and advocate unserious, ill-founded policies said to handle problems like those mentioned above. And all populists directly or indirectly want to weaken and abolish the institutional framework presented above that liberals favor. These institutions need to be secured and given a better defense in almost all democracies.

IMPROVE LIBERAL LITERACY

An important counterstrategy is therefore to explain to policymakers and the public how liberal institutions contribute to prosperity and welfare, as well as to meaning, community, and virtue. We have already noted that this is far from intuitive to most people how the spontaneous orders of liberal societies work. Unfortunately, this liberal illiteracy includes many politicians and academics, also within the field of economics.

Constitutional democracy, the rule of law, private property rights, and civil rights, including the freedom of speech, are all public goods. They benefit everyone in the longer run, while there often is a temptation for different interests—also non-populists—to free-ride and seek short-term benefits by limiting freedom or refraining from providing the necessary funding for the agencies that uphold them. If the police, the courts, and other parts of the judicial system do not get the support they need, law and order will deteriorate. The same is true for the freedom of the media and the democratic institutions themselves.

These are all basic institutional requirements for the market economy, civil society, and the open society in general. If this basic institutional framework is not defended and upheld, as in societies with rent-seeking, corruption, firm subsidies, over-regulation, bailouts, welfare dependency, crony capitalism, and the like, prosperity, civility, and the quality of life will deteriorate. And the political scene will lay wide open to a populist takeover.

But it is not only necessary to uphold the liberal institutions, the liberal economy and society with their spontaneous orders must be better explained. Adam Smith in *The Wealth of Nations* (1776) used the metaphor of the "invisible hand" to explain how the wealth of nations comes about. He argued that the market economy worked "as if" an invisible directed the butcher, carpenter, baker, industrialist, supplier, consumer, and other actors on the market to coordinate their behavior and act in a way that in the end benefitted everyone. But of course, there was no hand. It was the price mechanism, the profit motive, the competition, and the incentives created by the liberal institutions presented above that produced benevolent results. They arose as the unintended consequences of human action, but not of human design.

Less well-known and appreciated is that he first used the term the invisible hand in the *Theory of Moral Sentiments* (1759) where he shows that our moral judgments and actions are products of processes in civil society and social psychology. Social norms and individual virtues such as justice and benevolence arise, he argues, through interpersonal interactions and our ability to reflect on the impartiality of our actions and our feelings of sympathy of empathy with the situation of others. In this way we are often "led by an invisible hand...without knowing it, without intending it, [to] advance the interest of the society." (Smith 1759[1982]: IV.i.10).

The process he describes is similar to how, in the last chapter, we explained conditions necessary for the emergence and sustenance of social norms, namely informal, direct, long-lasting, and multi-dimensional relations within fairly small groups of people in communities in civil society.

While the benefits of the spontaneous orders of markets are well-known through empirical and historical research, there is also increasing evidence that the same is true of civil society. As shown by Elinor and Vincent Ostrom, and other scholars from the Bloomington school, communities and social norms in many situations make it possible to voluntarily solve various kinds of public goods problems and avoid the "tragedy of the commons" (Ostrom, 1990). Even in situations of natural disasters, this kind of decentralized, voluntary, and polycentric cooperation has been shown to be superior to centralized interventions. The role that government can play in the recovery is primarily to secure the basic liberal institutions such as private property rights (Chamlee-Wright & Storr, 2010).

Many, if not all, social and economic problems in today's democracies are likely to have been caused by policy interventions in markets and civil society. Non-classical liberal policymakers, for purportedly benevolent reasons, often favor policies that unintentionally destroy the spontaneous orders of liberal economies and societies.

One reason, as Bastiat (1850) famously argued, is that when people ponder the merits and demerits of government interventions, they too often are blind to the bulk of the interventions' consequences. Some are easily seen; others are not seen because they are indirect and occur over time. Often such unintended, unforeseen consequences are negative, they may even be contrary to the initial intentions.

Two typical examples are rent control and security on the job legislation. The former, intending to make housing cheaper and more available, leads to a lack in investments, ques, and shortages of housing, which often leads to demands for further regulation of input markets, subsidies, and further problems, rising costs in housing, etc., especially for the groups that originally was supposed to benefit. The latter, with the intention to make jobs safer and the risk of unemployment lower, often leads to the opposite through a less dynamic economy, a decreased willingness of employers to take the risk of employing, a dual labor market with insiders and outsiders, etc., in the end causing increased insecurity (Karlson, 1993 [2002, 2017]).

Good policies account both for the effects one can see and for those one must foresee. An implication of this analysis is that the demand for increased public spending and redistribution that frequently is heard, not only from left-wing populists and progressive politicians of various brands but also from populist scholars like Mounk (2018) and Fukuyama (2022), is likely to be misled. It may instead cause populism by undermining the liberal economy and society. As argued in Chapter 4, it should come as no surprise that welfare states are failing.

Understanding spontaneous orders requires education, it must be explained and communicated. Consequently, it is essential that resources are devoted to improving liberal literacy through public education but also through private initiatives. I shall return to this below.

SECURE A STRONG, LIMITED, AND DECENT STATE

Another important strategy is to secure a strong, limited, and decent state. In fact, a small but adequate state is likely to provide a better defense against populism than a larger, more interventionist state.

Classical liberals prefer limited government. That does not mean that they dislike or are against the state. What they want is a state that has the capacity to enforce the rule of law and the rights of individuals, uphold law and order, defend the country against foreign aggression, and support a limited set of genuinely collective goods.

As noted, there is some disagreement about what exactly should be included in this latter category, but almost all classical liberals would agree that education for all children, basic research, a well-functioning infrastructure, support for the vulnerable, weak, and unfortunate, various kinds of environmental protection, and perhaps other so-called "essential services" should be included. Galston (2005) has summarized this into what he calls "basic decency". But for example, Hayek favors public support for education and even an "equal minimum income for all" (Hayek, 1960: 427). Others would argue that also health care and other types of social services should be guaranteed, if not necessarily publicly provided, by the state. Such support, however, should have clear limits in order to avoid an unintended expansion of the state and infringements of the free market and civil society. Exactly where to draw the line would differ depending on the specific circumstances at hand. As shall be more fully explored below, classical liberals do not favor such systems because of social justice, but because of decency, and to promote social cohesion in society.

There are at least seven important arguments for why the government should be limited, which is not the case in most democracies today. The first well-known argument put forward by Nozick (1974) and other rights theorists is of course that a larger state may undermine the fundamental rights of individuals. He even views taxes beyond a certain level as being equivalent to slavery—you are forced to work for others without having given your support. While many classical liberals may not defend Nozick's account of rights, many would nevertheless agree that there are ethical limits to taxation (Buchanan, 1984).

A second, perhaps more general and in our context more relevant argument is that the state cannot know, and should not interfere with, the good of the individual. In contrast to populists of left and right, as well as socialists and conservatives, according to classical liberals, as far as possible the state should be neutral to the good life of its citizens. That is what liberty is about. A liberal society will be a pluralistic society with diverse values and different conceptions of the good. In fact, it can credibly be argued that only a liberal society with a liberal state can accommodate pluralism.

A third important argument is that a limited government gives larger room for markets and civil society, which will give higher prosperity and more innovation, but also stronger communities, voluntary organizations, social norms, and so on. This will strengthen the prospects for people to have lives with meaning, community, and virtue.

A fourth argument is that a limited government diminishes the amount of rent-seeking, lobbying, and corruption—the smaller the government the less interest for different special interests to try to influence it (Karlson, 1993 [2002, 2017]). The larger the government gets, the bigger the risk the public goods of the classical liberal institutions will be crowded out. A state that takes on too many functions faces the risk of creating political or policy failures that are more serious than the purported social and economic failures they may have been intended to fix (Karlson, 1993 [2002, 2017]; Buchanan & Tollison, 2009). The state needs to be limited and robust to be able to solve both incentive and information problems (Boettke & Leeson, 2004; Pennington, 2011).

A fifth fundamental argument is that a limited government with free markets and a civil society has epistemic advantages. In complex, culturally diverse societies a smaller, constitutionally bound state provides for better use of knowledge compared to its alternatives. Tebble (2016) critically examines multicultural, nationalist, and liberal egalitarian approaches and argues that an epistemic account of liberalism, that emphasizes social complexity rather than cultural diversity or homogeneity, is the most appropriate response to the question of justice in modern culturally diverse societies. Hence, society must ensure that all citizens have individual liberty to act upon their beliefs.

A sixth argument, made famous by Friedman and Friedman (1980), but also developed by Dahl (1983), is that a free society needs counterwailing powers in the private sector, in markets, and in civil society, to balance the power of the state. Without such resources, it is hard to see how a pluralist democracy and a strong, limited, and decent state could be sustained.

A seventh, and perhaps decisive, argument is that it directly limits the scope for populism. A liberal, constitutional democracy, obviously, makes it a lot harder for populists to achieve their authoritarian ambitions. With a division of power between the executive, legislative and judicial branches of government, independent power centers, and minority veto it will be harder for charismatic, plebiscitary leaders and their supporters to create a direct relationship with the 'people' by circumventing representative government, controlling courts, restricting media freedom, manipulating elections, etc.

It is also likely that the quality of political decisions will increase, as argued by Berggren and Karlson (2003), and will be improved with a liberal, constitutional democracy of the kind described above. The higher transaction costs regularly associated with the model of liberal democracy will often be a good thing—the deliberation introduced in governmental decision-making are likely to increase the quality of the political decisions. Moreover, it will not always be the case that liberal democracies have higher transaction costs than the more centralized, unitary, and populistic democracies. Given, of course, that the relevant institutions are wisely designed, a liberal democracy will have low decision costs, because of the partitioning of the domain of political decisions, and a high capacity to act in areas where it is appropriate, as well as a slow and more tedious decision process in areas where it is not appropriate to act without further deliberation. Overall, a strong, limited, and decent liberal democracy should, according to this analysis, be more in the long-term public interest of the voters.

Support Federalism and Decentralization

A related strategy against populism is to support federalism and decentralization. Federalism, or vertical division of power, has the advantage that decisions will be taken closer to the voters. The decentralization of political decision-making will lower the distance between the democratic representatives and their principals, the voters. It will increase institutional competition and make politicians more alert to the demands of the voters. And it will provide a stronger constitutional defense against unwanted or unintended centralization of politics (Karlson et al., 2008; Ostrom, 1973).

There are empirical results that support these views, even though a lot more work needs to be done in this area. For example, several studies show that the rate of inflation is lower, the size of the public sector smaller and the rule of law stronger in federal states than.

in unitary states. Certain types of referenda and bicameralism, furthermore, have a lowering impact on public spending. Factors such as bicameralism and presidentialism seem to contribute to higher wealth. Moreover, there are indications that the quality of democracy itself may be enhanced by an elaborate system of division of power. In his seminal study of thirty-six stable democracies Lijphart (1999: 301) found that, what he calls, consensus democracies (which in most respects correspond to Riker's liberal-democracy type) outperform majoritarian democracies concerning the quality of democracy and democratic representation.

Stimulate Social Mobility

Another quite different area, where institutions and policies should be improved to counter populism concerns social mobility and equality of opportunity. This may perhaps seem more controversial for some classical liberals, but not only are such policies likely to support equal dignity to the members of society, but they may also contribute to the social cohesion that the support for liberalism requires. A socially mobile society is moreover central to the liberal spirit.

However, equality of opportunity is not easily defined. Classical liberals favor procedural justice but are often critical of so-called social or distributional justice. In particular, the idea of equality of outcomes, or egalitarian social justice, is often advocated by left-wing populists, and is hardly compatible with a free society and a market economy (Hayek, 1976).

According to the procedural view of justice (Karlson, 1993 [2002, 2017]), all people should have equal rights regardless of gender, origin, and morality. That is what liberty and equal dignity are about. The rule of law and the equality of all before the law are central. From this perspective, the protection of economic, civil, and political rights and freedoms is the hallmark of a just society. From a procedural perspective also significant differences in income can be fair, as also Rawls (1970) acknowledged.

This does not mean that differences in income or wealth are uninteresting or unimportant. Large disparities in income and wealth can be detrimental to societal cohesion, individual health, and a range of other social problems (Wilkinson & Pickett, 2010). In addition, there is a risk that groups that perceive themselves as losers in such developments turn against established parties and elites and instead support different types of populist parties (Iversen & Soskice, 2019).

To make an open, liberal society inclusive and gain broad support, many liberals, therefore, promote policies that support social mobility. This includes basic social protection, education, and the like, or what I above have called decency. Even in this case, some redistribution and political interference are undeniably required, but to a much lesser extent in comparison with the egalitarian distributional claims. Promoting social mobility is more about compensating for poor conditions and lifting the foundations of all people, rather than seeking to reduce differences in themselves. Some differences, even major economic inequalities, can thus be fair.

The idea is that there are certain basic conditions or circumstances which the individual himself cannot influence or take responsibility for, and therefore should be reasonably equally distributed. While the result of what one can take responsibility for, such as work effort, skills, education, individual preferences, and the like, is something that the market and other societal processes are allowed to decide. Dworkin (1981), for example, analyzes what the individual himself has moral responsibility for and what fundamental circumstances can be considered to be beyond his or her control.

According to John Tomasi (2012) in Free Market Fairness, classical liberals should both be committed to limited government and the material betterment of the poor. It extends the notion that the protection of property and the promotion of real opportunity are indivisible goals. Similarly, Nick Cowen in Neoliberal Social Justice (2021) argues that the institutional framework of the market economy and the free society is probably the most important requirement for the achievement of real civic egalitarianism, rather than large-scale redistribution policies that most often result in cronyism and policy failures due to incentive and information problems.

It is not, of course, entirely simple to determine what should be included in these circumstances, and there is hardly any consensus among the above-mentioned thinkers, even if the starting point is somewhat similar. Biological differences, IQ, and similarity are circumstances that are difficult for the individual to influence, but they are also hard to influence through political efforts. And how do you draw the line towards aspects like self-drive, ambition, propensity towards risk, and savings, where the individual's choices and personal responsibility are greater but may still be influenced by upbringing and genetic factors? And how are the latter affected if we try to compensate for disadvantageous circumstances through redistribution policies and the like? There is a risk that the incentives for self-development will be taken away.

There is growing empirical literature that tries to measure how fair societies are from an equal opportunity perspective. This literature assumes that income inequality is fair if it has arisen as a result of toil, risk-taking, saving or education, but unfair if conditions beyond the control of individuals differed too much. While variables and methods used in the various studies vary greatly (Hufe et al., 2018), an important finding in (Checchi et al., 2010) is that education is what strengthens fair opportunities the most, or, conversely, reduces unfair income inequality. Also, in Hussey and Jetter (2016) the central finding is that education over time has become increasingly important in explaining income dispersion, although much else also comes into play.

One problem with these types of studies is that the results are entirely dependent on the variables used or available to measure fair opportunities. There is also a plethora of unobservable factors that can come into play. Moreover, as already mentioned, it is far from obvious what "circumstances" should be equal for everyone and what should be the individual's own responsibility.

An alternative option is to study intergenerational social mobility. By this is here meant the movement of individuals regarding occupation, social background or income compared to their parents. For example, the U.S. has a high level of mobility in terms of occupations and social class, but lower mobility in terms of income. European continental countries have low levels of mobility both in terms of occupation and income (Corak, 2013).

In a society that affirms equitable opportunities and social mobility, the education system has compensatory significance. That all citizens have the opportunity for high-quality education at an early age is crucial to be able to make responsible decisions later in life, develop their life projects, support themselves, earn money, start a family, etc. Education is also an area, alongside the fundamental liberal institutions discussed above, where politics really can play a constructive role, as already Smith (1776) recognized.

Unfortunately, politics does not deliver well in this regard in many countries. Probably, as argued above because the state has expanded way over its limits. Improving basic education for all is no doubt one of the most important counterstrategies against populism.

Strengthen Integration

There is also an apparent need in many democracies to strengthen the integration of immigrants. Most classical liberals favor the free movement of people across borders for many reasons, not the least because it promotes economic growth and prosperity for the world at large, but also in receiving countries (Caplan, 2019; Powell, 2015). Moreover, liberals embrace pluralism and cultural diversity. Even more important is that the right to exit one's country of residence is fundamental to liberty itself Kukathas (2003). Also, for those already living in liberal democracies and open societies. As argued by Kukathas (2021), there is moreover a risk that restrictions on mobility and border controls infringe the liberties of the very citizens they aim to protect.

However, also in tolerant, pluralistic societies, immigrants need to be sufficiently integrated economic-socially and culturally to support social cohesion and to avoid social and economic problems. Labor market participation is here crucial to the development of language and social skills. In fact, labor immigration may also support the integration of refugees and asylum seekers.

As we saw in Chapter 4, the public perceptions of the size of immigration differ considerably from reality. In countries like Hungary and Poland, where the right-wing populist rhetoric around the threat of immigrants is especially intensive, the actual number of immigrants is very low. This is not very surprising given Allport's (1954) well-tested interpersonal contact theory which states that direct interpersonal contact with members of minority and other social groups is one of the most effective ways to reduce stereotyping, prejudice, and intergroup conflict.

In an interesting study, Fleming et al. (2018) used the Migrant Acceptance Index (Espiova et al., 2018) to see whether direct interpersonal contact with migrants reduces stereotyping and prejudice against them. The index is based on three questions that were asked in 138 countries. The questions ask whether people think migrants living in their country, becoming their neighbors, and marrying into their families are good things or bad things. Several EU countries are among the least accepting countries of migrants globally including Hungary, Croatia, Latvia, and Slovakia. Many of the most-accepting countries have a long reputation as receiving countries for migrants—like the U.S., Australia, Canada, and New Zealand. The results show a near-universal relationship between self-reported interpersonal contact with migrants and personal attitudes toward them.

It is interesting to note that these Anglo-Saxon countries differ from many others in at least two ways: their labor market models are more flexible, and they have prioritized labor migrants as well as refugees and asylum seekers. Canada, Australia, and New Zealand all welcome labor migrants through scoring or merit systems. In Canada, immigrants from countries with a high level of education are prioritized and each individual is tested against the conditions for self-sufficiency. The applicant's education, language, and work experience are valued in relation to Canada's need for labor. The applicant must first achieve some minimum standards in the form of having graduated from high school or equivalent, demonstrating proficiency in English or French, worked at least one year continuously in a qualified profession, and possessing sufficient financial means to be able to support themselves and their family during the start-up period. The applicant is then scored based on other variables such as education, age, work experience and whether the applicant already has relatives in place (Canadim, 2022). Australia introduced a similar scoring system in 1989 and New Zealand in 1991. These, unlike Canada, have chosen to more take into account in the scoring system the identified shortage of occupations in the labor market. In Australia, applicants who have a profession that is on a list of highly qualified shortage occupations receive a work permit (Emilsson & Magnusson, 2015).

Labor immigration is important in two respects. First, labor immigration can lead to more support for immigration policy among the population. In Australia, for example, refugee immigration is a minus item for government finances over a 10-year period, but immigration policy overall contributes positively to government finances because labor immigration is so profitable and extensive (Cully, 2011). Second, there are several indirect effects that labor migrants can contribute to improving integration for refugees.

Since it is likely that refugees and labor migrants often live in the same neighborhoods (especially in the early years of the country), labor migrants could have positive spillover effects on refugees who have traditionally found it more difficult to enter the labor market and society. Åslund and Fredriksson (2009) show that lower levels of welfare dependence in refugees' immediate areas reduce the risk of them taking out income support themselves. Similar conclusions can be drawn for the integration of children and adolescents. Edin et al. (2003) show that a higher proportion of immigrants in the residential area leads to poorer school results for refugees' children, but that a higher proportion of their compatriots who are highly educated in the immediate area improves school results, especially for boys. Thus, if labor migration leads to a higher degree of education in areas with a high proportion of immigrants, this could help to improve the school performance of refugee children.

The other way that Anglo-Saxon countries differ from many other developed countries concerns their labor market models (Karlson & Lindberg, 2012). Compared to the other European models the Anglo-Saxon model has a more market-based view of the labor market. But it still provides for flexicurity, although with lower compensation rates for unemployment (Eamets et al., 2009). There is only a low level of government involvement and less comprehensive welfare policies. The coverage of collective agreements is low, just as the levels of membership in unions and employers' organizations. Moreover, the model is based on the system of common law rather than on legislation. At the heart of this model, alongside a small amount of regulation, is the notion of a flexible labor market ruled by the price mechanism. In this model, there is greater freedom provided to individual employers to hire and fire personnel, and the freedom to set pay and employment terms and conditions. Consequently, this greater flexibility makes it easier for low-skilled immigrants to be integrated into the labor market, and hence their ability to support themselves and their families, which diminishes all kinds of social problems and welfare costs. Also, on-the-job training will support language and social skills, all to the benefit of integration.

Hence, to support the integration of immigrants in general, also low-skilled asylum seekers, labor immigration but also institutions that lowers the barriers to the labor market are important, rather than subsidies and welfare benefits. Again, the classical liberal institutions with a strong limited, and decent state that protect individual and minority rights and support the creation of jobs and prosperity are the way forward.

Restore Public Discourse

A last critical area for reform that needs to be raised concerns the role digital social media seems to have in the deterioration of public discourse and the rise of populism, as we saw in Chapter 4. While I am no expert in the topic of algorithms and the business models of digital platforms, it clearly is a problem if media consumers increasingly, especially in younger generations, are exposed only to information that confirms their preexisting values and beliefs. It will undermine the ability to respectfully disagree and the quality of public discourse; the "tribal mind" may get hold.

How to fix this is not without complications, however, since digital media at the same time is a fantastic technology that makes information and new knowledge available to almost everyone, everywhere, any time. In that sense, it is genuinely democracy-enhancing. Moreover, it is a young technology that is still evolving through competitive technological advances.

For example, algorithms could just as well be designed to provide upgraded digital "town squares" that encourage consensus rather than division, downgrade misinformation and deep fakes, and support high-quality public discourse. Supporting such a development should be in the interest of both users and platform businesses. The public is also likely to become more accustomed to using social and digital media for their long-term benefit.

While some form of regulation—possibly upgrading similar regulations that apply to traditional media such that platforms to a larger extent are made responsible for the content on their sites, but also giving people more control over their personal data—is likely to come, the downside is similar to what was discussed above in the context of the benefits of limited government. The risk is that policy failures are created that are worse than the problem that the regulation was supposed to fix in the first place. The regulatory process could, which is not unlikely in the present political environment, be captured by special interests or the populist politicians themselves, stifling innovation, and free speech.

One way to think about this could be to be inspired by the German ordoliberal tradition, which emphasizes the government's role to provide, protect and enforce non-discriminatory general rules of the game for economic and social interaction, especially to uphold competition, without intervening in the process itself or becoming a player itself (Dold & Krieger, 2019; Kolev et al., 2020). Especially the distinction between market-conforming and non-conforming state intervention holds some lessons in this area as well (Siems & Schnyder, 2014). "Public discourse-conforming rules" that protect and enforce non-discriminatory general rules of the game may be needed for digital media as well.

REFERENCES

Åslund, O., & Fredriksson, P. (2009). Peer effects in welfare dependence: quasi-experimental evidence. *The Journal of Human Resources, 44*(3), 798–825.

Allport, G. W. (1954). *The nature of prejudice.* Perseus Books.

Bastiat, F. (1850). *Ce qu'on voit et ce qu'on ne voit pas, ou l'Économie politique en une leçon.* Par M. F. Bastiat, Représentant du peuple à l'Assemblée nationale, Membre correspondant de l'Institut (Paris: Guillaumin, 1850).

Berggren, N., & Karlson, N. (2003). Constitutionalism, division of power and transaction costs. *Public Choice, 117*(1–2), 99–124.

Boettke, P. J., & Leeson, P. T. (2004). Liberalism, socialism, and robust political economy. *Journal of Markets and Morality, 7*(1), 99–111.

Buchanan, J. (1984). The ethical limits of taxation. *The Scandinavian Journal of Economics, 86*(2), 102–114.

Buchanan, J., & Tollison, R. (2009). *The Theory of public choice—II.* The University of Michigan Press.

Canadim (2022). How to immigrate to Canada. *Canadian Immigration Law Firm.* https://www.canadim.com/immigrate/. Gathered January 13, 2023.

Caplan, B. (2019). *Open borders: the science and ethics of immigration.* First Second.

Chamlee-Wright, E., & Storr, V. H. (Eds.). (2010). *The political economy of hurricane Katrina and community rebound*. Edward Elgar Publishing.

Checchi, D., Peragine, V., & Serlenga, L. (2010). *Fair and unfair income inequalities in Europe*. IZA Discussion Paper No. 5025. Bonn: IZA - Institute of Labor Economics.

Corak, M. (2013). Income inequality, equality of opportunity, and intergenerational mobility. *Journal of Economic Perspectives, 27*(3), 79–102.

Cowen, N. (2021). *Neoliberal social justice: Rawls unveiled*. Edward Elgar.

Cully, M. (2011). Skilled migration selection policies: Recent Australian reforms. *Migration Policy Practice, 1*(1), 4–7.

Dahl, R. A. (1983). *Dilemmas of pluralist democracy: Autonomy vs. control*. Yale University Press.

Dold, M., & Krieger, T. (2019). Ordoliberalism and European economic policy: An introduction. In M. Dold & T. Krieger (Eds.), *Ordoliberalism and European economic policy: Between realpolitik and economic utopia* (pp. 1–20). Routledge.

Dworkin, R. (1981). What is equality? Part 2: Equality of resources. *Philosophy & Public Affairs, 10*(4), 283–345.

Eamets, R., Philips, K., Alloya, J., & Krillo, K. (2009). *Benchmarking EU countries against Danish flexicurity model*. University of Tartu.

Edin, P.-A., Fredriksson, P., & Åslund, O. (2003). Ethnic enclaves and the economic success of immigrants—evidence from a natural experiment. *Quarterly Journal of Economics, 118*(1), 329–357.

Emilsson, H., & Magnusson, K. (2015). Högkvalificerad arbetskraftsinvandring till Sverige. In C. Calleman, P. Herzfeld Olsson (eds.), *Arbetskraft från hela världen: hur blev det med 2008 års reform?* (pp. 72–113). Delmi.

Espiova, N., Pugliese, A., & Ray. J. (2018, December 18). Revisiting the most- and Least-accepting countries for migrants. *Gallup*. https://news.gallup.com/opinion/gallup/245528/revisiting-least-accepting-countries-migrants.aspx. Gathered January 13, 2023.

Fleming, J. H., Esipova, N., Pugliese, A., Ray, J., & Srinivasan, R. (2018). DATA-SURVEY: Migrant acceptance index: A global examination of the relationship between interpersonal contact and attitudes toward migrants. *Border Crossing, 8*(1), 103–132.

Friedman, M., & Friedman, R. D. (1980). *Free to choose*. Harcourt Brace Jovanovich.

Fukuyama, F. (1989). The end of history? *The National Interest, 16*(Summer 1989): 3–18.

Fukuyama, F. (1992). *The end of history and the last man*. Free Press.

Fukuyama, F. (2022). *Liberalism and its discontents*. Profile Books.

Galston, W. A. (2005). *The practice of liberal pluralism*. Cambridge University Press.

Hayek, F. A. (1976). *Law, legislation and liberty, Vol 2: The Mirage of Social Justice*. Routledge & Kegan Paul.

Hayek, F. A. (1960). *The constitution of liberty*. University of Chicago Press.

Hufe, P., Kanbur, R.. & Peichl, A. (2018). *Measuring Unfair Inequality: Reconciling Equality of Opportunity and Freedom from Poverty*. IZA Discussion Paper No. 11601. Bonn: IZA—Institute of Labor Economics.

Hussey, A., & Jetter, M. (2016). Long term trends in fair and unfair inequality in the United States. *Applied Economics, 49*(12), 1147–1163.

Iversen, T., & Soskice, D. (2019). The Politics of the Knowledge Economy and the Rise of Populism. In *Democracy and Prosperity* (pp. 216–256). Princeton University Press.

Karlson, N. (1993 [2002, 2017]). *The state of state. An inquiry concerning the role of invisible hands in politics and civil society*. Almquist & Wiksell International. (Also published by Transaction Press, New Brunswick & London, with a new preface, 2002, and by Routledge, London 2017).

Karlson, N., Berggren, N., Bergh, N., Erlingsson, G., & Lindberg, H. (2008). *Institutionell konkurrens*. Underlagsrapport 4. Globaliseringsrådet. Stockholm: Regeringskansliet.

Karlson, N., & Lindberg, H. (2012). *Labour markets at a crossroads: Causes of change, challenges and need to reform*. Cambridge Scholars Publishing.

Kolev, S., Goldschmidt, N., & Hesse, J. O. (2020). Debating liberalism: Walter Eucken, FA Hayek and the early history of the Mont Pèlerin Society. *The Review of Austrian Economics, 33*(4), 433–463.

Kukathas, C. (2003). *The liberal archipelago*. Oxford University Press.

Kukathas, C. (2021). *Immigration and freedom*. Princeton University Press.

Lijphart, A. (1999). *Patterns of democracy: Government forms and performance in thirty-six countries*. Yale University Press.

Mounk, Y. (2018). *The People vs. Democracy: why our freedom is in danger and how to save it*. Harvard University Press.

Nozick, R. (1974). *Anarchy, state, and utopia*. John Wiley & Sons.

Ostrom, E. (1990). *Governing the commons: The evolution of institutions for collective action*. Cambridge University Press.

Ostrom, V. (1973). Can federalism make a difference? *Publius, 3*(2), 197–237.

Pennington, M. (2011). *Robust political economy: Classical liberalism and the future of public policy*. Edward Elgar.

Popper, K. (1945). *The open society and its enemies*. Routledge.

Powell, B. (Ed.). (2015). *The economics of immigration: Market-Based approaches, social science, and public policy*. Oxford University Press.

Rawls, J. (1971). *A theory of justice*. Harvard University Press, Belknap Press.

Siems, M., & Schnyder, G. (2014). Ordoliberal lessons for economic stability: Different kinds of regulation. *Not More Regulation. Governance, 27*(3), 377–396.

Smith, A. (1757[1982]). *The theory of moral sentiments*. Liberty Classics.
Smith, A. (1776). *An inquiry into the nature and causes of the wealth of nations: Volume One*. printed for W. Strahan; and T. Cadell.
Tebble, A. J. (2016). *Epistemic liberalism: A defence*. Routledge.
Tomasi, J. (2012). *Free market fairness*. Princeton University Press.
Wilkinson, R., & Pickett, K. (2010). *The spirit level: Why equality is better for everyone*. Bloomsbury Press.

CHAPTER 9

Embrace and Promote the Liberal Spirit

Abstract In this chapter a third kind of counterstrategy against populism is presented and discussed, namely, to embrace and promote the liberal spirit. Building on the tradition from von Humboldt and Mill, I argue that it is possible to develop a liberal politics of recognition and identity that gives credit to the different lifestyles and conceptions of a good life that characterize a liberal society. Such politics could offer emancipation, meaning, and community, a sense of purpose and belonging, and human flourishing in a broad sense. In addition, the need for a liberal collective legitimizing identity and for liberal narratives are discussed.

Keywords Counterstrategy against populism · The liberal spirit · Liberal identity politics · Human flourishing · Communitarian critique · Liberal institutions · Liberal narratives

A third major type of counterstrategy to fight back against the populists is to develop and embrace the less often emphasized dimension or facet of classical liberalism, namely the spirit of liberalism. Rational arguments and facts for how to improve institutional arrangements and the functioning of the liberal economy and society are not likely to be able to do the full job. As already Aristotle argued, to persuade you need to convince the audience in three different areas: logos, pathos, and ethos. Logos

N. Karlson, *Reviving Classical Liberalism Against Populism*,
Palgrave Studies in Classical Liberalism,
https://doi.org/10.1007/978-3-031-49074-3_9

concerns rational argumentation; pathos appeals to emotions; and ethos emphasizes the importance of character. Liberals should become better to appeal to pathos and ethos. As Jonatan Mercer observes, often "feeling is believing because people use emotions as evidence" (Mercer, 2010: 1).

In Chapter 5 I argued humans have a quest for meaning and community that populism has exploited through a collectivistic identity politics. Most people are seeking meaning and want to engage in purposes that give fulfillment. They also have a quest for community and belonging. And many devote their lives to forming their character and developing virtues that contribute to human flourishing. It should be possible to advance a liberal politics of recognition that gives credit to the different lifestyles and conceptions of a good life that characterizes a liberal society. Such politics could offer emancipation, meaning, and community, a sense of purpose and belonging, and human flourishing in a broad sense, that should be attractive to large parts of society.

The populist collectivistic identity politics is based on antagonism and constructed existential enemies that appeal to the tribal mind of many people. As argued in Chapter 4, such an intuitive part of the human psyche is a latent trait of human psychology. In the terminology of Kahneman, these more intuitive systems can take over the rational, slower, effortful, and more controlled system, making us use different simplifying heuristics, such as the ones populism offers. Latent tribal instincts may be activated, and subversive conspiracies may even develop into "parasites of mind". This deliberate polarization of society is at the core of populist identity politics. It is also a politics that in the long run may undermine social norms and virtues.

This means that liberals need to take on the challenging work to explain why and how a liberal system is superior, not only in terms of economic outcomes, but to a good society in more general terms, emotionally and character-wise, including the recognition of different lifestyles, cultures, and identities, i.e., with an appeal to pathos and ethos.

MEANING, COMMUNITY, AND VIRTUE IN A LIBERAL SOCIETY

Liberalism may seem to lack an identity politics. But as shall be argued, this is not necessarily so. It would be a politics of pluralism and tolerance, that recognizes the value of different personal, social, and normative identities, and equal dignity and respect. This is where the spirit of liberalism comes in. A core idea in liberalism is that every individual should have the right to decide over his or her own life, her identity, what is meaningful, which communities to belong to, and to develop her character and virtues. There is an important liberal tradition, at least from Wilhelm von Humboldt and John Stuart Mill and onwards, that argues that the perhaps most important argument in favor of a liberal society is that it is a prerequisite to individual self-development and human flourishing.

Many liberals thus believe that self-development, not to be confused with selfishness, is one of the most important values or goals of such a liberal society. In *The Limits of State Action* Wilhelm von Humboldt (1969 [1852]: 16), written already in 1791–1792, argued that:

> The true end of Man, or that which is prescribed by the eternal and immutable dictates of reason, and not suggested by vague and transient desires, is the highest and most harmonious development of his powers to a complete and consistent whole. Freedom is the first and indispensable condition that the possibility of such a development presupposes.

Similarly, developing one's abilities to the fullest, according to John Stuart Mill, should be the goal of human endeavor. In *On Liberty* (1859 [1975]: 56) he emphasized that:

> Among the works of man, which human life is rightly employed in perfecting and beautifying, the first in importance surely is man himself.

Mill also famously argued that some projects are more worthy than others and that liberty is needed precisely to find out what is valuable in life – we learn about the good. This is how the right to liberty promotes the good.

Both also emphasized that self-development was not only dependent on liberty but also on a pluralistic society—the consequence of liberty—where different experiences and examples of how to live exist. And both Humboldt and Mill, again, argued that education was a prerequisite to human flourishing. Moreover, self-development involved the development of character and sociability, something that also would benefit society at large (Mautner, 2020; Valls, 1999). In the terminology used in a Chapter 5, this means that they argued that meaning, community, and virtue would flourish in a liberal society.

In the last decades, there has been a renewed interest in Aristotelian virtue ethics and human flourishing, in general, but also in the relationship between liberalism and human flourishing. One of the best examples from a classical liberal perspective is Douglas B. Rasmussen's and Douglas J. Den Uyl's *Norms of liberty: a perfectionist basis for non-perfectionist politics* (2005) where they argue why individual rights of liberty are prerequisites for moral pluralism and human flourishing understood to be an inclusive, individualized, agent-relative, social, and self-directed activity. On their account, human flourishing is objective, plural and profoundly social. In their view, "individualistic perfectionism," supports liberal, non-perfectionist, or neutral, politics, or a classical liberal state, as described in the last chapter.

Others, such as Joseph Raz, in the *Morality of Freedom* (1986), defend an autonomy-based perfectionism. A good life is that of autonomous persons creating their own lives through progressive choices from a multitude of valuable options. In his view, this makes it legitimate for the state to seek to promote the conditions for individual autonomy, or if you want, self-development or even human flourishing. Amartya Sen and Martha Nussbaum, on their hand, discuss the importance of what they call" basic capabilities" for human flourishing (Nussbaum, 2011). These are the capabilities that they argue should be secured by the state and fairly distributed to support human flourishing. None of these latter authors thus do defend a totally neutral state, and at least Sen and Nussbaum cannot be considered to be classical liberals. But again, classical liberals themselves disagree about the exact limits of state action when it comes to measures to support a decent and cohesive society. Concerning human flourishing, however, most would agree that education, skills development, and perhaps also basic health care have key roles.

A Politics of Tolerance, Recognition, and Human Flourishing

From these perspectives on human flourishing, a more elaborate classical liberal identity politics could be developed to be part of the answer for how to fight back against the populists. Such a liberal politics of recognition could provide a liberal ethos or spirit that gives credit and respect to the different identities, lifestyles, and conceptions of a good life that characterizes a liberal society.

Such identity politics is a politics of pluralism of personal and social identities. Importantly, it is a politics that respects and recognizes the diverse ways people choose to live their lives. The classical liberal institutions provide the necessary framework for individual self-development, meaning, community, and virtue, where people themselves can find out what is valuable. Without freedom and pluralism, it is not possible to learn from experience and the example of others. Neither is it possible to find opportunities of doing and engage in meaningful projects that have a purpose, some mission, or cause. In such a society family, friends, and clubs in civil society, moreover, provide communities that form the basis for social cohesion and social norms, which also may be supported by polices that support social mobility. And without individual liberty, it is hard to see how individuals could develop their character and virtue. The liberal rights protect the conditions under which individuals can pursue their flourishing, but they do not, of course, guarantee success.

It is fundamental, thus, to distinguish between the classical liberal institutional requirements and the results of these procedures. In markets and civil society, individuals can pursue their own goals without being subservient to centralized political authority. People can even pursue mutually contradictory purposes and values, without being restricted by some majority view. As put by Kymlicka (1989), liberals argue for the right of moral independence not because our goals are arbitrary, but precisely because our goals can be wrong, and because we can revise and improve them.

The communitarians philosophers mentioned in the last chapter argued that liberalism is excessively individualistic and atomistic, and not only lacks an understanding of the importance of the social foundation that communities and collective belonging provide for virtues and a good life but also that liberalism undermines the kind of identity that defines a good society. They argue that the self, the identity of a person, always is embedded or situated and that liberals have a too limited view of what an individual is. This may well be true of some economists within the neo-classical tradition, liberal or not, at least in their economic models, where an individual is nothing else than a preference function that should be maximized. The same goes for the narrow Randian conception of human motivation. There may also have been a one-sidedness by liberals on the necessary procedural or institutional requirements of a liberal society, such as the rule of law, pluralism, constitutional democracy, and limited government. But it is a mistake to think that liberals do not understand that identities are socially embedded. As emphasized above, liberalism is more than its procedures.

The communitarians have addressed this kind of critique against the procedural theory of justice of John Rawls' *A Theory of Justice* (1971) where he uses an abstract and stylized "original position", in a similar way as Locke and Kant, to derive his principles of justice. However, what they tend to forget is that this position where the individual is stripped of many of his or her real-world characteristics, is just a construct, a model, used to ensure impartiality (Karlson, 1993 [2002, 2017]) and to identify morally relevant aspects (Fairfield, 2000) for political principles, not for society at large. Rawls himself had a broad understanding of the importance of the social embeddedness of the individual:

> No doubt even the concepts that we use to describe our plans and situation, and even to give voice to our personal wants and purposes, often presuppose a social wetting as well as a system of belief and thought that are the outcome of the collective efforts of a long tradition. (Rawls 1971: 522)

As I will argue below, in a similar way as Fairfield (2000), classical liberals have no problems with accepting that individuals are socially embedded or that they form identities based on meaning, community and virtue. In fact, it is the institutional structure of liberal society that makes such identities possible. In this sense, in a liberal society, identities emerge as a kind of spontaneous order.

Let us start with meaning. In a liberal, pluralistic society there are ample opportunities for doing and engaging in things that have a purpose, some mission, or cause. As illustrated by Humboldt and Mill above, self-authorship of one's life project, as Tomasi (2012) puts it, is at the heart of liberalism. Such a life project need not be self-interested but can just as often have the ambition to promote causes that are larger than oneself, for example, the development of virtuous behavior, helping others, promoting justice, and contributing to human flourishing, to use the Aristotelian expression.

Another example is entrepreneurship, in which to succeed largely depends on the ability to promote the interests of others – how else can you succeed in markets based on voluntary contracts? As an entrepreneur, you always care about employees, customers, and suppliers; otherwise, you will soon be out of business (Karlson et al., 2015; Storr, 2008).

Perhaps the most meaningful projects in a liberal society are tied to being a parent, having a job, engaging in voluntary organizations of civil society, or having a hobby. Or for that matter, to engage in public discourse and politics to try to improve the institutions of society.

The same is true about community. It is a myth that the individualism of liberalism should be atomistic or anti-community. Family, friends, and clubs provide communities that form the basis for social cohesion and social norms in a pluralistic civil society. To most individuals, this is where their real sense of belonging and identity, purpose in life, pride, and self-esteem is created and upheld. A liberal economist and social philosopher with this perspective was Wilhelm Röpke (1960) who favored a "humane economy" with decentralized decision-making, small communities, and free markets, where moral behavior, virtues, accountability, and personal responsibility would flourish. Notably, he was also critical of the welfare state that he feared would destroy the communities of civil society. Similar arguments are made by Botteke (2021) and McCloskey (2019).

Robert Nisbet (1953), as well as Robert Putnam (1993) and many others, have argued that a dynamic civil society with strong communities, separate from the state, fulfill numerous roles: it makes gives a sense of belonging and community, it creates social capital, it makes cooperation and the production of local public good or club goods possible (Buchanan, 1965), it stimulates responsible behavior and social trust (Uslaner, 2002). Admittedly there may also be communities where family, friends, and clubs promote hierarchical subordination and the like. But what ultimately makes civil society liberal is pluralism and the possibility of exit as an option (if not without costs) (Kukathas, 2003).

The strongest case for a classical liberal identity politics concerns the role of virtues (Berkowitz, 1999). Without individual liberty, it is hard to see how individuals could develop their character and virtues. Without learning from voluntary practical actions and reflection about one's experiences, and the pluralistic experiences of others, human flourishing is simply not possible, just as many liberal thinkers have argued. Both Humboldt and Mill meant that the value of liberty primarily was that it enabled individuals to develop their character through experience and practical wisdom. The same is true for Rasmussen and Den Uyl referred to above.

A Collective Legitimizing Identity?

What liberalism may seem to have a harder time offering is the sense of collectivist belonging that the populists may provide to their followers. Or what perhaps a Medieval city or society could offer through religion, myths, superstitions, and other non-rational collectivist beliefs, as the communitarians seem to want. Or what paternalistic socialist, conservative, or nationalist welfare states try to offer. Liberals' belief in pluralism, tolerance, and equal rights means that there will be all kinds of different and competing opinions about the good and what a good life is. That is the point of liberty and what a liberal politics of identity is about.

But liberalism may also need a collective legitimizing identity, to use Castells' term (Castells, 2004), to protect itself. All liberals can offer, it may seem, is a kind of collectivist identity based on the liberal institutional framework and procedures themselves, such as the safeguard of liberty, individual rights, the rule of law, and constitutional democracy. This idea has been called constitutional patriotism by Habermas (1996). Müller (2008) has argued that such an attachment is necessary in multicultural societies to enable and uphold a liberal democratic form of rule that free and equal citizens can justify to each other.

Others argue that a kind of liberal nationalism is needed, that individuals need a national identity to lead meaningful, autonomous lives, and that democratic polities need national identity to function properly (Kymlicka, 1995; Miller, 1995; Tamir, 1993). It is thus not an argument only saying that nation-states historically have played a role in establishing liberal institutions, but rather that liberal multicultural democracies polities need a national identity to be sustained. As argued by Tamir (1993), membership in a liberal nation not only involves rights but also special obligations and responsibilities towards each other, obligations that may not apply to non-members.

A consequence of liberal nationalism is that the state may not really be said to be fully neutral anymore to different views of the good life that its citizens may hold. An actual example of this is the French concept of *laïcité*, which originally emerged as a way, similar to the US constitution, to guarantee a strict separation between the state and religion, but that over time has evolved into a concept whose underlying purpose is to secure critical characteristics of French culture, such as banning the wearing of Muslim burkas (Leane, 2011).

A third kind of argument, developed already by Mill, is that liberalism may need a new kind of liberal religion, which he calls "the religion of humanity", to sustain the virtues, values, and beliefs that a liberal society needs to be sustained (Mill, 1969). Even someone like Buchanan, a professed atheist, has approved of a similar idea. In the paper titled "The Soul of Classical liberalism", already mentioned above, he refers to the need for a "classical-liberal predisposition" and defines it as "an attitude in which others are viewed as moral equals and thereby deserving of equal respect, consideration and ultimately equal treatment" (Buchanan, 2005: 101).

In my view, it is the liberal spirit, and its emphasis on human flourishing, the third dimension of liberalism presented above, rather than religion or nationalism, formulated as a classical liberal identity politics that could offer such a collective legitimizing identity. What liberals can offer is a sense of belonging to an open, prosperous, and pluralistic society, a culture where people tolerate, respect, enjoy and recognize the different values, lifestyles, and conceptions of the good of others and themselves. It is a society that celebrates science, free speech, and rational discourse. It is not a utopia, but to defend liberalism in this broad sense against the populist threat is undoubtedly a meaningful cause that is larger than the individual herself. It is a cause that should have the potential to mobilize a critical mass of support against infringements of freedom. It is also a cause that is more inclusive, more encompassing, and more sustainable in the long run than the collectivistic identity that the populists pretend to offer.

To achieve the support of this is of course easier said than done. For classical liberalism to create reasonable collective legitimizing identity would at least require liberal narratives.

CREATE LIBERAL NARRATIVES

An important counterstrategy against the populists is thus also to create more and better narratives of why and how liberalism and liberal institutions contribute to a good society. This would need to be narratives that combine ethos, pathos, and logos.

There is a need to revive and create liberal narratives that not only support markets and wealth creation, but that also cherish civil society and the liberal spirit in all its dimensions. These narratives need to be inclusive, rather than divisive and show how individuals and other actors in markets and civil society can flourish in liberal societies. They need to embrace tolerance and equal respect for others, despite differing views about the good.

Deirdre McCloskey (2016, 2019) and others have made an excellent job of explaining how classical liberal ideas, virtues, institutions, and policies have contributed to, what she has termed, *The Great Enrichment*. But it is just as important to explain how classical liberalism has contributed to what may be called *The Great Emancipation*. Liberalism is essentially just that, a story of liberation for the many. Or even better *The Great Flourishing*, of how the classical liberal ideas, institutions, and spirit have contributed to human flourishing.

A narrative is basically a story, a series of related events or experiences. It is a way of presenting connected events to tell a good story. Narratives normally have a certain structure comprised of actors, events, plot, time, setting, and space. It connects apparently unconnected phenomena around some causal transformation (Miskimmon et al., 2013).

The populist strategy, rhetorical style, and discursive frame with the 'us-versus-them' logic is of course a narrative, constructed to create polarization and support for autocratization. In the words of postmodernists and critical theorists, it is a metanarrative or grand narrative, that claims to explain economic, social, and political developments and to create meaning by connecting disperse events and phenomena. It is not about facts, but about emotions, resentment, and fear. It serves to delegitimize liberalism, modernity, and the ideas of the Enlightenment.

History, however, is full of real-world stories and actual liberal narratives of the emancipation of ordinary people. Examples are the abolition of serfdom and slavery, as well the fight for Jewish emancipation and the women's liberation movement. During the late eighteenth and nineteenth centuries liberalism became the preeminent reform movement in Europe, combining liberal rights and the opening of free markets. For example, Adam Smith not only supported free trade and free markets but also attacked serfdom and slavery.

From the last quarter of the eighteenth century into the second half of the nineteenth century, emancipation brought an end to serfdom in all European states, but Hungary and Russia as late as the 1860s. Brazil became the last nation in the Americas to abolish slavery in 1888, and it may still exist in parts of Africa and the Middle East (Eltis et al., 2017). Similar, long-term processes, combing active support for equal rights and market-driven change, largely fits the history of Jewish emancipation

(Sorkin, 2019) and the women's emancipation movement (Evans, 1977; Paletschek and Pietrow-Ennker, 2003). Liberals should devote more time and energy to developing these and similar processes into narratives.

Today history is seldom written from a classical liberal perspective. As argued Douma and Magness (2018), classical liberals represent a small minority among academic history departments, which tend to be dominated by Marxist, postmodernist, critical theorist, or conservative schools. Consequently, the importance of liberal ideas and institutions, and perhaps in particular free markets (Hayek, 1954), tend largely to be unappreciated when history is taught and written.

In more popular culture—in movies and novels—the situation is similar, even though there are exceptions that come to mind. For example, we have classics that make us understand totalitarians systems way better than most academic attempts, like One Day in the Life of Ivan Denisovich by Aleksander Solzhenitsyn, Darkness at Noon by Arthur Koestler, The Trial by Franz Kafka, Fahrenheit 451 by Ray Bradbury, Animal Farm and 1984 by Ernest Hemingway, and The Handmaid's Tale by Margaret Atwood, just to mention a few.

While several of these books have been made into movies, just as Isaac Asimov's Foundation series that also deals with tyranny, there are other movie narratives that capture the spirit of classical liberalism's strive for liberty and emancipation, like George Lucas' Star Wars and J. R. R. Tolkien's Lord of the Ring series, the later of course first published as novels.

But none of them fully explain the benefits and the human flourishing of a liberal order. The same is largely true for the novels of Ayn Rand, but for a slightly different reason. While doing a good job at exposing the negative effects of collectivist ideas, her conception of human motivation and development is, in my view, way too narrow and self-oriented to fit the understanding of human flourishing presented above.

Hence, there is work to be done for the defenders of liberty, and not only politicians but just as important actors in markets and civil society, in media, gaming, universities, and cultural institutions. Liberalism needs heroes, stories of emancipation and flourishing, and epic narratives of hope that capture the imagination, and that also show that populism is a tragedy.

REFERENCES

Berkowitz, P. (1999). *Virtue and the making of modern liberalism*. Princeton University Press.

Boettke, P. (2021). *The struggle for a better world*. Advanced studies in political economy serie. Mercatus center, George Mason University.

Buchanan, J. (1965). An Economic Theory of Clubs. Economica. *New Series, 32*(125), 1–14.

Buchanan, J. (2005). Afraid to be free: Dependency as desideratum. *Public Choice, 124*(1–2), 19–31.

Castells, M. (2004). *The power of identity*. (2nd ed.). Blackwell Publishing.

Douma, M., & Magness, P. (Eds.) (2018). *What is classical liberal history?* Lexington Books.

Eltis, D., Engerman, S. L., Drescher, S., & Richardson D. (Eds.) (2017). *The cambridge world history of slavery. Volume 4: AD 1804–AD 2016*. Cambridge University Press.

Evans, R. J. (1977). *The feminists. Women's emancipation movements in Europe, America and Australasia 1840–1920*. Routledge.

Fairfield, P. (2000). *Moral selfhood in the liberal tradition: The politics of individuality*. University of Toronto Press.

Habermas, J. (1996). *Between facts and norms: Contribution to a discourse theory of law and democracy*. MIT Press.

Hayek, F. A. (Ed.) (1954). *Capitalism and the historians*. University of Chicago Press.

Karlson, N. (1993 [2002, 2017]). *The state of state. An inquiry concerning the role of invisible hands in politics and civil society*. Almquist & Wiksell International. (Also published by Transaction Press, New Brunswick & London, with a new preface, 2002, and by Routledge, London 2017).

Karlson, N., Wennberg, K., & Norek, M. (2015). *Virtues in entrepreneurship*. Ratio och Publit förlag.

Kukathas, C. (2003). *The liberal archipelago*. Oxford University Press.

Kymlicka, W. (1989). *Liberalism, community and culture*. Clarendon Press.

Kymlicka, W. (1995). *Multicultural citizenship*. Oxford University Press.

Leane, G. (2011). Rights of ethnic minorities in liberal democracies: Has France gone too far in banning muslim women from wearing the burka? *Human Rights Quarterly, 33*(4), 1032–1061.

Mautner, M. (2020). *Human flourishing, liberal theory, and the arts*. Routledge.

McCloskey, D. (2016). *Bourgeois equality: How ideas, not capital or institutions, enriched the worlds*. University of Chicago Press.

McCloskey, D. (2019). *Why liberalism works: How true liberal values produce a freer, more equal, prosperous world for all*. Yale University Press.

Mercer, J. (2010). Emotional beliefs. *International Organization, 64*(1), 1–31.

Mill, J. S. (1969). *The collected works of John Stuart Mill, Volume X—Essays on ethics, religion, and society*, Robson, J. M. (Eds.), University of Toronto Press.

Mill, J. S. (1859 [1975]). *On liberty*, Spitz, D. (Eds.), Norton and Co.

Miller, D. (1995). *On nationality*. Oxford University Press.

Miskimmon, A., O'Loughlin, B., & Roselle, L. (2013). *Strategic narratives: Communication power and the new world order*. Routledge.

Müller, J. W. (2008). A general theory of constitutional patriotism. *International Journal of Constitutional Law, 6*(1), 72–95.

Nisbet, R. (1953). *The quest for community: A study in the ethics of order and freedom*. Oxford University Press.

Nussbaum, M. (2011). *Creating capabilities*. The Belknap Press of Harvard University Press.

Paletschek, S., & Pietrow-Ennker, B. (Eds.). (2003). *Women's emancipation movements in the nineteenth century*. Stanford University Press.

Putnam, R. (1993). *Making democracy work: Civic traditions in modern Italy*. Princeton University Press.

Rasmussen, D. B., & Den Uyl, D. J. (2005). *Norms of liberty: A perfectionist basis for non-perfectionist politics*. Penn State University Press.

Rawls, J. (1971). *A theory of justice*. Harvard University Press.

Raz, J. (1986). *The morality of freedom*. Oxford University Press.

Röpke, W. (1960). *A humane economy*. Henry Regnery Company.

Sorkin, D. (2019). *Jewish emancipation: A history across five centuries*. Princeton University Press.

Storr, V. H. (2008). The market as a social space: On the meaningful extraeconomic conversations that can occur in markets. *The Review of Austrian Economics, 21*, 135–150.

Tamir, Y. (1993). *Liberal nationalism*. Princeton University Press.

Tomasi, J. (2012). *Free market fairness*. Princeton University Press.

Uslaner, E. (2002). *The moral foundation of trust*. Cambridge University Press.

Valls, A. (1999). Self-development and the liberal state: The cases of John Stuart Mill and Wilhelm von Humboldt. *The Review of Politics, 61*(2), 251–274.

von Humboldt, W. (1969) [1852]). Cambridge University Press.

CHAPTER 10

Develop Liberal Statecraft

Abstract This chapter presents a fourth kind of counterstrategy against populism. I argue that a liberal statecraft should be developed that not only promote a liberal economy but also a civil and open society, and perhaps most importantly the liberal spirit. All the strategies presented in earlier chapters should be included. Its success requires the conquering of the idea arena, the promotion of liberal policy entrepreneurs, and the investment in power resources that can change institutions and policies. To embrace and promote the liberal spirit as a collective legitimizing identity is a central task for liberal statecraft.

Keywords Counterstrategy against populism · Liberal statecraft · Policy entrepreneurs · Polycentric effort · Power resources

The last kind of counterstrategy against populism I wish to advance is to develop liberal statecraft. Liberal statecraft can be defined as the art of governing a country well, i.e., successfully promoting liberal institutions and policies that are welfare-enhancing and make society freer (Karlson, 2018). It is a statecraft that promotes not only a liberal economy but just as important a civil and open society, and perhaps most importantly the liberal spirit. Liberal statecraft thus concerns the long-term institutional development of society, not short-term electoral or parliamentary tactics.

N. Karlson, *Reviving Classical Liberalism Against Populism*,
Palgrave Studies in Classical Liberalism,
https://doi.org/10.1007/978-3-031-49074-3_10

Populism, as should be obvious, is the opposite of statecraft however one wants to define it. To promote unserious and ill-founded policy solutions to complex social and economic problems to get elected cannot be considered a case of statesmanship or policy improvement in a welfare-enhancing direction. Neither can the deliberate polarization of society through populist rhetorical and discourse framing, demonizing opponents, etc.

Liberal statecraft, to promote institutional change in a liberal direction, requires the ability to conquer the idea arena, the promotion of liberal policy entrepreneurs, and the investment in power resources that actually can change institutions and policies.

The strategies necessary to achieve this, as argued in the previous chapters, include:

- the exposure of the populist strategies and consequences,
- the defense and development of liberal institutions,
- the improvement of liberal literacy,
- the securement of a strong, limited, and decent state,
- the support of federalism and decentralization,
- the stimulation of social mobility,
- the implementation of high-quality basic education,
- the strengthening of integration,
- the restoration of public discourse,
- the embracement and promotion of the liberal spirit, and
- the creation of liberal narratives.

Importantly, these strategies not only involve rational argumentation but also arguments that appeal to emotions and arguments about the ethos or spirit of a liberal society. They are not only about enrichment, but also about emancipation, meaning, community, virtue, and human flourishing. Obviously, the demanding work of policy improvement must be done, just as the liberal institutions must be defended and explained. A strong, limited, and decent state is what is required, including the promotion of social mobility, the implementation of high-quality basic education to all, the strengthening of integration, and the restoration of public discourse, as well as reforms in other areas. Let me also emphasize all these reforms to a considerable extent need to be adapted to the local conditions in the relevant societies and polities in question. And the spontaneous orders in markets and civil society need to be explained and communicated.

But as we saw in Chapters 4 and 5, one of the key factors behind the rise of populism is a cultural backlash that appeals to the identity of people. Therefore, it is not enough for liberals to appeal to interests, they also must appeal to the identity of people. It is necessary to formulate and advance a liberal politics of recognition and respect. Such an appeal could be based on the importance of human flourishing and the liberal spirit, as explained above. Civil society, with families, voluntary organizations, clubs, etc., the market economy, and an open, pluralistic society provide better opportunities for this than any alternative system. This must be explained and communicated in such a way that voters and ordinary people can feel respect and pride in their choices. Here liberal narratives, also supporting a liberal collective legitimizing identity, have important roles. To embrace and promote the liberal spirit as a collective legitimizing identity is a central task for liberal statecraft.

Liberal statecraft as described above cannot be limited to the activities of a single person, as in populist charismatic leadership. Liberal statecraft concerns the broader process, where different actors with distinct roles in different spheres of society contribute to the process. Liberal statecraft is a "polycentric" effort where many different actors and policy entrepreneurs need to be involved. Intensive public discourse and "polycentric" learning are likely to be required to develop liberal ideas (Karlson, 2018).

To successfully implement these kinds of strategies requires a broad spectrum of skills, skills, broader than those held by economists or other typical experts. For example, it is not so surprising that the successful presidents Ronald Reagan in the US and Volodymyr Zelensky in Ukraine both have a background in television and the movie industry. Reagan had appeared in more than 50 movies before he entered a political career (Reagan, 2011). Zelensky, a political novice, had made a career as a director, entertainer, and comedian on both television and in movies with a significant online following before he entered the presidential race in Ukraine in 2019 (Britannica, 2022). While surely having good analytical and rational skills, both the rhetorical use of pathos and ethos came naturally. The same is true for Churchill, with a long-term background as a journalist and author of history. It is also interesting to note that all three advanced an agenda of hope, despite the harsh times they faced (see e.g., White, 2008). And they all appealed to the efforts of ordinary citizens in an effort to revive liberty, prosperity, and human flourishing. They flaunted the 'virtuous', in harsh contrast to today's populists.

Note, moreover, that they all faced serious external threats, in the latter two cases virtually existential threats, which they used to mobilize the support they needed to promote liberal policies. In most cases, however, such "help" is not available since the threat from populists most often comes from within one's society. This means that leadership of the kind the three examples give are the exception. In most democracies, liberal statecraft will be a process in which many different actors with different skills will have to participate. It is a collaborative and virtuous effort that requires courage and fortitude. And it is a task that requires substantial resources in terms of skills, people, and money, an investment with huge future returns.

REFERENCES

Britannica. (2022). *Volodymyr zelensky, president of Ukraine.* https://www.britannica.com/biography/Volodymyr-Zelensky

Karlson, N. (2018). *Statecraft and liberal reform in advanced democracies.* Palgrave MacMillan.

Reagan, R. (2011). *An American life: The autobiography.* Simon & Schuster

White, J. (2008, October 13). In dark times, Reagan ran on optimism. *NBC News.* https://www.nbcnews.com/id/wbna27117516. Gathered January 13, 2023.

CHAPTER 11

A Classical Liberal Revival

Abstract The last chapter summarizes my conclusions by asking for a revival of liberalism itself. While populism for several reasons may be self-defeating in the longer run, the costs may be exceedingly high. Classical liberalism is a much richer tradition than the strawman of neoliberalism that many left-wing populists and social scientists have constructed. It is not only able to offer prosperity and security, but also a sense of belonging and community that is superior to what the right-wing populists and nationalists are asking for. It is a tradition that needs to be developed and revitalized.

Keywords Liberal revival · The spirit of classical liberalism · Policy development · Policy entrepreneurs · Polycentric effort

The ideas and institutions of classical liberalism created the modern world. The liberty, prosperity, and human flourishing that the world has experienced during the last 200 years would not have happened without institutions that secure individual liberty, equal rights, the market economy, free trade, freedom of association, the rule of law, pluralism, constitutional democracy, and limited government. The liberal economy and society have created wealth, welfare, voluntary cooperation, social cohesion, and

N. Karlson, *Reviving Classical Liberalism Against Populism*,
Palgrave Studies in Classical Liberalism,
https://doi.org/10.1007/978-3-031-49074-3_11

emancipation for humans worldwide on a scale unprecedented in human history.

Today these achievements are threatened by a worldwide populist wave that undermines liberty, free markets, and an open society. While there are other kinds of authoritarian regimes, populism is a threat that has emerged within democracies. What has happened is that liberal institutions fundamental to both markets and democracies, as well as civil society – the rule of law, independent courts, and different civic and political liberties—have been weakened or started to crumble. The number of liberal democracies has been falling for the last two decades and a large majority of the world's population today lives in different sorts of autocracies.

The success of populism can largely be explained by the divisive activist ideas they base their policies on, ideas originating in the works of Rousseau, Nietzsche, Heidegger, and Schmitt, later developed within post-modernism and critical theory.

The populists use a distinct rhetorical style or discursive frame to deliberately create the polarization of society into an'us versus them' antagonism, using emotional arguments and framing to create anger and moral outrage towards opponents and their supporters. Often a real or imagined economic or social crisis of some kind, increasing uncertainty, is used to trigger such tribal sentiments. The use of unserious and ill-founded policy solutions to complex social and economic problems is most often also part of populist strategies. When in power, the autocratic institutional orientation of populism is manifested in the gradual decline of the democratic, open society, rather than open coups, a process of creeping autocratization. There are both left—and right-wing versions of these populist strategies that share the same structure.

Populism from left to right is a kind of collectivistic identity politics. It appeals to the'people' by offering a sense of belonging, to the nation, class, history, social status, religion, or some other trait, and by offering a worthy purpose and meaning, namely, to defend the people against enemies and threatening others, both constructed by the populist themselves.

This kind of politics is the opposite of classical liberalism. It is contrary to freedom, to liberal institutions, to the liberal society with markets and civil society, to pluralism, and to the liberal spirit that cherishes optimism and human flourishing. Therefore, liberals need to fight back. The world will not change for the better unless liberals do. Liberals must develop and revitalize their own ideas, beliefs, and values to battle populism, just as in previous times in history.

Writing in 2023, the autocratic threats from Putin's Russia and Xi Jinping's China may have triggered an increased awareness among democracies of the West about the necessity to defend their liberal institutions and societies. But even though external threats (ironically similar to the populist logic of 'us-versus-them') may help to mobilize support, such threats cannot do the job itself and are surely insufficient in the longer run.

It may also be argued, as in Weyland (2022), that populism is somehow self-defeating, as some of the more recent elections in countries like the US and Brazil may indicate. He argues that the personalistic, plebiscitary leaders of populist movements tend to make mistakes and misdeeds that undermine the support of both the masses and important special interests and other established political actors, which make checks and balances and external constraints set in. While this may well be true in some cases, in other cases –countries like Venezuela and Hungary come to mind—the process of creeping autocratization may have gone too far to be reversed easily. Also, other populists, perhaps with an opposite ideological orientation, as frequently has been the case in Latin America, may gain power instead.

There is, however, another, perhaps more fundamental reason populism may be self-defeating. Recall the analysis in Chapter 5 where it was argued that small-scale communities like those of families, friends, and clubs were prerequisites for the emergence and sustenance of social norms and that such norms could be upheld also in larger groups or collectives if they were internalized. But when the underlying communities disappeared, the social norms in the collectives would eventually disappear as well. And so will the collective sense of belonging that the populists offer. The same may also be true of the personal virtues that are learned by practicing them, in markets and civil society, and by reflecting on these practices, throughout life—they may also be undermined. A society without either social norms or personal virtues is not likely to be attractive to anyone.

Instead of passively awaiting the collapse, a better and more long-term solution to the populist threats to liberty, free markets, and the open society involves a revitalization of liberalism itself. Classical liberalism is a much richer tradition than the strawman of neoliberalism that many left-wing populists and social scientists have constructed. It is not only able to offer prosperity and security, but also a sense of belonging and community that is superior to what the right-wing populists and nationalists are asking for. It is a tradition that can and need to be developed and revived.

Such a revival is only partly a question of better policy responses to changes in economic and social conditions affecting voters. Or a better defense of the liberal institutions and policies that actually are welfare enhancing. Modern liberals have largely neglected that humans have a quest for meaning, community, belonging, identity, and a purpose in life, that we are meaning-searching, meaning-creating animals. Hence, it is also necessary to revitalize the soul or the spirit of classical liberalism. In addition, liberals need to invest more resources in policy entrepreneurs and political leaders that have the skills and ambitions to articulate and promote liberal policies in the political process.

In the previous chapter about classical liberal statecraft several strategies for how to fight back against populism have been suggested. These include the exposure of the populist strategies to make the public and voters aware of the deliberate manipulation that lies behind the strategies used by populists and the negative consequences that follow for society at large, and in the end for the supporters of the populists themselves. Liberals also need to be better at defending and developing liberal institutions and policies. When economic and social conditions change, many institutions and policies need to change as well. In general, liberals must be better at defending and explaining why a strong, limited, and decent state is preferable to its alternatives, and how the liberal institutions it upholds produce spontaneous orders in markets and civil society. But there are also specific policies that need to be advanced, such as the promotion of social mobility, the implementation of high-quality basic education for all, the strengthening of integration, and the restoration of public discourse.

But rational argumentation and policy improvement will not be enough. Liberals also need to appeal to emotions and character by advancing a liberal politics of identity, a politics that shows that a liberal society can offer meaning, community, belonging, identity, and emancipation. It is an embedded liberal politics that emphasizes self-development and human flourishing. More and better narratives of why and how liberalism and liberal institutions contribute to a good society need to be created to achieve this, narratives that combine ethos, pathos, and logos.

Lastly, I have suggested that liberals should develop liberal statecraft by conquering the idea arena, promoting liberal policy entrepreneurs, and investing in power resources that can change institutions and policies. This is a polycentric effort where many different actors and policy entrepreneurs need to be involved. The promotion of the liberal spirit is central to liberal statecraft.

The defense of liberty, free markets, and an open society is a long-term project that requires many different skills and virtues. It is difficult, but no doubt possible, and with great potential to all. The cost may be exceedingly high if we do not try.

Reference

Weyland, K. (2022). How populism dies: Political weaknesses of personalistic plebiscitarian leadership. *Political Science Quarterly, 137*(1), 9–42.

INDEX

A
Activist, 2, 4, 12, 38, 48, 51, 52, 122
Alternative für Deutschland, AFD, 14
Anti-pluralism, 14, 15
Aristotle, 58, 101
Asia, 2, 22, 23, 39
Austerity, 30, 32, 36
Australia, 28, 94, 95
Austria, 14, 32, 33, 60
Authoritarian, 16, 22–24, 35, 70, 74,
    89, 122
  authoritarian pandemic, 2
  authoritarian predisposition, 37, 40,
    41
Autocracy, 2, 23, 122
Autocratic, 2, 3, 12, 15–17, 27, 30,
    47, 62, 68, 79, 122, 123
Autocratization, v, 3, 4, 8, 10, 18,
    28, 29, 41, 49, 80, 81, 110, 122,
    123
Automation, 30, 32

B
Backsliding, 21, 23, 28, 67

Beliefs, 4, 8, 28–30, 35, 37, 41, 56,
    68, 74, 75, 89, 96, 108, 109,
    123
Berlin, Isiah, 1, 68, 70, 74
Berlusconi, Silvio, 40
Bloomington school, 86
Bolsonaro, Jair, 8, 14
Buchanan, James, 30, 60, 68, 70, 72,
    88, 107, 109

C
Canada, 49, 94
Capitalist, 13, 14, 16
Character, 3, 53, 57–59, 61, 73, 102,
    103, 105, 107, 108, 124
Charismatic leadership, 18, 39, 117
Chavez, Hugo, 8, 11, 12, 62
China, 2, 12, 24, 30, 32, 62, 123
Civil rights, 3, 48, 85
Civil society, 3, 11, 12, 16, 24, 51,
    56, 70–73, 75, 85–89, 105, 107,
    109–111, 117, 122–124
Classical liberal
  classical liberal ideas, 69, 110

classical liberal identity politics, 104, 107, 109
classical liberal revival, 69, 124
Classical liberalism, v, 3, 4, 48, 68–73, 75, 101, 109–111, 121–124
Collectivistic, 56, 60, 109
  collectivistic identity politics, v, 2, 4, 41, 48, 59, 62, 68, 81, 102, 122
Communism, 2
Community, 13, 16, 35, 36, 39, 49, 53, 54, 56–61, 68, 72, 74, 84, 86, 88, 102, 103, 105–107, 116, 123, 124
Competition, 3, 13, 16, 34, 85, 90, 97
Conservatism, 8
Constitutional constraints, 10, 18, 69
Constitutional democracy, 3, 61, 71, 85, 89, 105, 108, 121
Corbyn, Jeremy, 14
Corruption, 34, 84, 85, 88
Cosmopolitan, 13, 14, 57
Counterstrategies, v, 2, 4, 75, 83, 93
Courts, 11, 16, 18, 24, 68, 80, 85, 89, 122
Crises, 8, 30–32, 36, 40, 83
Critical theory, 4, 12, 48, 51, 52, 122
Cuba, 2, 24
Cultural backlash, 35, 36, 117
Culture, 13, 23, 33, 35, 36, 51, 52, 54, 57, 62, 102, 108, 109, 111

D
Dahl, Robert, 24, 89
Decency, 87, 88, 91
Decentralization, 90, 116
Decent state, 87, 89, 96, 116, 124
Demagogues, 11
Democracy
  constitutional democracy, 3, 61, 71, 85, 89, 105, 108, 121

illiberal democracy, 16, 18, 69
level of democracy, 1, 23
liberal democracy, 8, 11, 15, 16, 27, 71, 75, 80, 89
Democratic backsliding, 23, 28, 67
Dictatorial, 2
Dictatorship, 51
Dignity, 3, 48, 49, 55, 61, 70, 90, 91, 102
Discursive frame, 2, 3, 17, 47, 49, 67, 110, 122
Diversity, 3, 37, 73, 75, 89, 93
Divisive, 2, 4, 12, 48, 109, 122
Duterte, Rodrigo, 11, 39, 40

E
Eastern Europe, 16, 23, 32, 34, 40
Echo chambers, 38, 41
Economic conditions, 28, 30, 35
Economic freedom, 24, 72
Elections, 9, 12, 15–18, 22–24, 52, 69, 71, 89, 123
Elite, 13, 34
Emancipation, 74, 102, 110, 111
Emotions, 3, 12, 49, 57, 102, 110, 116, 124
Entrepreneurship, 3, 73, 106
Equality, 12, 35, 48, 52, 61, 90, 91
Equality of opportunity, 90, 91
Erdoğan, Recep Tayyip, 14, 16, 39
Establishment, 10, 18, 52, 69, 72
Ethnic, 13, 14, 53
Ethos, 3, 69, 73, 101, 102, 104, 109, 116, 117, 124
Europe, 2, 22, 36, 39, 60, 110
European Union, EU, 10, 13, 33, 34, 94
Existential enemies, 102

F
Fake news, 12, 18, 41, 50, 52, 69

Families, 3, 56, 72, 94, 96, 117, 123
Far-right parties, 31
Fascism, 2, 62, 72
Federalism, 71, 90, 116
Fidesz, 14, 15
Filter bubbles, 38
France, 14, 32, 33, 61
Frankfurter school, 50, 51
Freedom, 3, 18, 23, 24, 37, 38,
    69–72, 80, 85, 89, 91, 95, 103,
    105, 109, 121, 122
  economic freedom, 24, 72
  freedom of the press, 80
Free markets, v, 2, 3, 21, 23, 31, 70,
    72, 89, 107, 110, 111, 122, 123,
    125
Freiheitliche Partei Österreichs, FPÖ,
    14, 33
Friedman, Milton, 24, 70, 72, 89
Fujimori, Alberto, 39
Fukuyama, Francis, 31, 49, 52, 54,
    84, 87

G
Galston, William, 10, 11, 70, 73, 74,
    87
General will, 10, 12, 15, 49
Globalization, 13, 14, 30–33, 35, 40,
    49
Greece, 14, 15

H
Haidt, Jonathan, 37, 39
Hayek, F.A., 24, 70, 72, 73, 87, 91,
    111
Heidegger, Martin, 4, 12, 48–51, 122
Human flourishing, 3, 74, 102–104,
    106, 107, 109–111, 117, 118,
    121, 122, 124
Human nature, 8, 37, 41

I
Ideas, v, 2, 4, 10, 12, 18, 28–30, 35,
    38–41, 48–52, 54, 60, 61,
    68–70, 73, 75, 110, 111, 117,
    121–123
Identity
  identity politics, 13, 36, 48–50, 52,
    59, 60, 102, 105
  legitimizing identity, 108, 109, 117
Identity politics
  collectivistic identity politics, v, 2,
    4, 41, 48, 59, 62, 68, 81, 102,
    122
  liberal identity politics, 104, 107,
    109
  populist identity politics, 61, 62,
    102
Ideology, 2, 7, 54, 60
Illiberal, 16, 18, 22, 69
Immigration, 31, 33, 35, 40, 80, 84,
    93–96
India, 15, 32, 60
Individual rights, 12, 104, 108
Inequality, 9, 13, 14, 30–33, 35, 40,
    92
Institution, v, 2–4, 9, 10, 12, 14, 16,
    24, 28–30, 34, 36, 39, 69, 70,
    72, 73, 75, 83–86, 88–90, 93,
    96, 105, 107–111, 115, 116,
    121–125
Institutional change, 2, 3, 28–30, 39,
    40, 116
Integration, 32, 84, 93, 95, 96, 116,
    124
International Monetary Fund, IMF, 9,
    13
International trade, 30, 32
Islam, 13
Islamist, 15
Italy, 14, 15, 33, 34, 40

J
Jews, 10, 13

L
Laclau, Ernesto, 51, 52
Latin America, 2, 8, 16
Leaders, 11, 16, 21, 22, 30, 33, 34,
    37–41, 48, 49, 61, 69, 89, 123,
    124
Leadership, 12, 18, 39, 117, 118
Legitimacy, 16, 49
Legitimizing identity, 108, 109, 117
LGBTQ, 13, 48
Liberal
    liberal counterstrategies, 4
    liberal democracy, 8, 11, 15, 16,
        27, 71, 75, 80, 89
    liberal economy, 4, 75, 85, 87,
        101, 115, 121
    liberal elites, 35
    liberal institutions, v, 2, 4, 24, 72,
        73, 75, 83–86, 88, 93, 96,
        105, 108, 109, 115, 116,
        122–124
    liberal literacy, 87, 116
    liberal narratives, v, 109, 110, 116,
        117
    liberal politics of identity, 3, 108,
        124
    liberal potentials, 4, 75
    liberal predicaments, 4, 68
    liberal society, 3, 60, 70, 72, 88,
        91, 102–107, 109, 116, 122,
        124
    liberal spirit, v, 3, 4, 69, 73–75, 90,
        109, 115–117, 122, 125
    liberal statecraft, v, 3, 4, 75,
        115–118, 124, 125
Liberalism
    classical liberalism, v, 3, 4, 48,
        68–73, 75, 101, 109–111,
        121–124

    neoliberalism, 12, 13, 31, 70, 80,
        123
    social liberalism, 3, 71
Liberalization, 1, 24
Likud, 15
Limited government, 3, 70, 71, 73,
    75, 87–89, 92, 97, 105, 121
Locke, John, 50, 69, 106

M
Maduro, Nicolás, 8, 62
Markets, 1, 3, 8, 12, 13, 21, 23, 24,
    31, 51, 60, 61, 70–73, 75, 86,
    88, 89, 105, 106, 109–111, 117,
    122–125
Marxist, 14, 62, 111
McCloskey, Deirdre, 29, 32, 58, 73,
    107, 110
Meaning, 4, 36, 39, 54–57, 60, 61,
    68, 74, 84, 88, 102, 103, 105,
    106, 110, 116, 122, 124
Media, 11–14, 16, 18, 24, 38, 39,
    41, 52, 61, 62, 69, 79, 80, 85,
    89, 96, 97, 111
Mill, John Stuart, 70, 74, 103, 106,
    107, 109
Minority rights, 3, 18, 22, 49, 69, 96
Money, 93, 118
    sound money, 3
Mont Pelerin, 70
Mouffe, Chantal, 51, 52
Mounk, Yascha, 30, 38, 87
Mudde, Cas, 10, 16, 31, 34
Multiculturalism, 35, 48, 49, 52, 80

N
Narratives, 3, 12, 18, 47, 51, 52, 58,
    60–62, 80, 111, 124
    liberal narratives, v, 109, 110, 116,
        117

Nationalism, 9, 13, 14, 49, 54, 57, 108, 109
Nationalist, 14, 32, 48, 57, 60, 62, 89, 108, 124
National Rally (National Front), 14
Neoliberalism, 12, 13, 31, 70, 80, 123
New Zealand, 94
Nietzsche, Friedrich, 4, 12, 48–51, 54, 122
Norms, 33, 36, 56–58, 61, 72, 73, 81, 85, 86, 88, 102, 105, 107, 123
North Korea, 2, 24, 62
Nozick, Robert, 70, 88

O

Open society, v, 3, 4, 8, 9, 15, 16, 18, 21, 24, 27, 28, 62, 67, 72, 80, 85, 115, 122, 123, 125
Orbán, Victor, 16, 39
Ordoliberal, 97
Ostrom, Elenor, 56, 86

P

Perspectivism, 50
Peru, 39
Philippines, 11, 40
Plebiscitarian, 24
Pluralism, 3, 22, 23, 61, 71, 72, 88, 93, 102, 104, 105, 107, 108, 121, 122
Podemos, 14, 15
Poland, 14, 32, 33, 35, 60, 94
Polarization, 2, 8, 10, 13, 18, 28, 37–41, 50, 69, 79–81, 102, 110, 116, 122
Polarized, 38, 41, 52, 61, 80
Policy, 8, 17, 18, 22, 28, 31, 68, 86, 116

policy entrepreneurs, 4, 28, 30, 39, 40, 69, 116, 117, 124, 125
policy failure, 29, 30, 34, 84, 88, 92, 97
Polycentric, 4, 86, 117, 125
Popper, Karl, 24, 70, 72, 84
Populism
  defining characteristics, 2, 3, 8
  left-wing populism, 4, 12, 13, 48
  right-wing populism, 4, 12, 13, 48, 62
Populist
  populist ideas, v, 2, 3, 29, 30, 38, 40, 41, 68
  populist rhetoric, 21, 23, 27, 28, 31, 33, 37, 41, 50, 94
  populist strategies, 3, 4, 12, 13, 15, 17, 18, 23, 49, 68, 75, 80, 83, 116, 122, 124
Post-modernism, 4, 12, 48, 50–52, 122
Predicaments, 4, 68
Private property, 24, 71, 72, 85, 86
Private sphere, 3, 71
Property rights, 3, 24, 70–72, 85, 86
Prosperity, 32, 72–75, 84, 85, 88, 93, 96, 118, 121, 124
Protectionism, 9, 13, 14, 61
Psychology, 3, 37, 51, 53, 55, 59, 85, 102
Public discourse, 38, 68, 84, 96, 97, 107, 116, 117, 124
Putin, Vladimir, 12, 62, 123

R

Rational argument, 2, 12, 18, 80, 101
Rationality, 49, 72
Rawls, John, 91, 106
Recognition, 12, 18, 39, 48, 49, 54, 57, 59, 61, 73, 80, 102
  politics of recognition, 48, 61, 102, 104, 117

Redistribution, 8, 13, 14, 32, 40, 61, 71, 87, 91, 92
Resentment, 48, 49, 110
  politics of resentment, 48
Revival, v, 4
  classical liberal revival, 69, 124
Rhetoric, 16, 21, 22, 27–29, 31, 33, 37, 41, 50, 62, 94
Rhetorical style, 2, 3, 12, 14, 15, 17, 23, 27, 39, 41, 47, 49, 67, 80, 110, 122
Rights
  civil rights, 3, 48, 85
  minority rights, 3, 18, 22, 49, 69, 96
  property rights, 3, 24, 70–72, 85, 86
Rodrik, Dani, 8, 30, 35
Rousseau, Jean-Jacques, 4, 10, 48, 49, 51, 122
Rule of law, 1, 3, 18, 24, 34, 61, 69, 70, 72, 85, 87, 90, 91, 105, 108, 121, 122
Russia, 2, 12, 24, 62, 110, 123

S
Sanders, Bernie, 14
Schmitt, Carl, 4, 12, 48–52, 122
Self-authorship, 3, 73, 106
Shklar, Judith, 70, 71
Smith, Adam, 50, 58, 59, 70, 72, 85, 86, 93, 110
Social
  social conditions, 28–30, 34, 40, 68, 83, 84, 124
  social justice, 88, 91
  social liberal, 22
  social media, 11, 38, 39, 41, 61, 62, 79, 96
  social mobility, 84, 90, 91, 93, 105, 116, 124

social norms, 33, 56–58, 61, 72, 73, 81, 85, 86, 88, 102, 105, 107, 123
Socialism, 2, 8, 72
Socialist, 12, 14, 22, 62, 74, 88, 108
Spain, 14, 15, 49
Spontaneous order, 73, 85–87, 106, 117, 124
State, 2, 12–16, 18, 23, 31, 35, 49, 51, 60, 61, 69–72, 87–89, 93, 97, 104, 107, 108, 116, 124
Statecraft, v, 3, 4, 75, 115–118, 124, 125
Strategy, 10, 13, 35, 50, 81, 87, 90, 110
Sweden, v, 14, 28, 33
Swedish Democrats, 14
Syrzia, 15

T
Taylor, Charles, 54, 59
Tolerance, 3, 37, 72–75, 102, 108, 110
Tomasi, John, 92, 106
Totalitarian, 2
Tribalism, 10, 40
Trump, Donald, 11, 14, 39, 40, 49, 80

U
Unemployment, 30, 32, 86, 95
United Kingdom Independence Party, UKIP, 14
United States, US, 2, 11, 13, 14, 32, 33, 35, 36, 39, 40, 48, 74, 80, 108, 117, 123
Us-versus-them, 10–13, 18, 22, 39, 52, 54, 69, 80, 110, 122, 123

V

Values, 4, 8, 12–16, 23, 28–30, 33, 35, 39, 41, 55, 60, 61, 68–70, 75, 88, 96, 103, 105, 109, 123

Venezuela, 8, 11, 62, 123

Vietnam, 24

Virtue, 3, 54, 57–59, 61, 72, 73, 81, 84, 85, 88, 102–107, 109, 110, 116, 123, 125

Volonté general, 10, 49, 61, 80

von Humboldt, Wilhelm, 70, 103

Voter support, 21, 22

W

Welfare, 13–15, 28, 31, 32, 40, 60, 61, 73, 84, 85, 87, 95, 96, 107, 108, 115, 121, 124

  welfare programs, 31, 32, 40, 61

  welfare system, 13, 14, 33

Western Europe, 22

Working class, 13, 14

World Bank, 10, 13